A-GAME
POKER

Master The Mental Game, Create A Winning Mindset, &
Dominate The Modern Poker Game

ELLIOT ROE
& RYAN CARTER

ELLIOT ROE & RYAN CARTER

Printed Worldwide
First Printing 2023
First Edition 2023
ISBN: 979-8-9897162-0-3
10 9 8 7 6 5 4 3 2 1

Names:	Roe, Elliot, author. | Carter, Ryan (Ryan S.), author. | Galfond, Phil, writer of foreword.
Title:	A-game poker : master the mental game, ccreate a winning mindset, & dominate the modern poker game / Elliot Roe & Ryan Carter ; foreword by Phil Galfond.
Description:	Draper, UT : Mindset Coach, [2023]
Identifiers:	ISBN: 979-8-9897162-0-3 (paperback) | 979-8-9897162-1-0 (kindle)
Subjects:	LCSH: Poker--Handbooks, manuals, etc. | Poker--Psychological aspects. | Poker--Competitions--Psychological aspects. | Poker--Tournaments--Psychological aspects. | Poker--Anecdotes. | Poker players--Psychological aspects. | Poker players--Anecdotes. | Poker players--Vocational guidance.
Classification:	LCC: GV1251 .R64 2023 | DDC: 795.412--dc23

Any product mentioned in this book does not imply endorsement of or affiliation with that product by the author or publisher. The conversations and stories in the book are based on the author's recollections, though they are not intended to represent verbatim transcripts. Rather, the author has retold them in a way that communicates the spirit of what was said and happened.

MINDSET COACH

Mindset Coach LLC
138 E 12300 S Unit #781
Draper UT 84020
United States
AGamePoker.com
Send feedback to hello@agamepoker.com

*For Ali, Launa and Winter, thanks for giving me
a reason to improve everyday.*

—

*To Adrienne, Carrick, Cian, and Caitlin, for making today
(and everyday) a wonderful day.*

How To Get Your Bonuses & Resources

Before you read a single page of this book, your buying decision is already a +EV one.

In addition to the book, your purchase makes you eligible to claim a suite of bonus content, resources, and discounts exclusively for A-Game Players.

Throughout this book, I'll ask you to complete specific exercises designed to take you from information to implementation. I want you to get maximum value from this book, which means completing the exercises and taking action on the protocols.

To make sure you go to the resources page and download those exercises and resources, I've added some valuable bonus content, as well as significant discounts for my flagship course, The A-Game Poker Masterclass, my Primed Mind app, and other products and services that complement the content of this book and help take your game to the next level.

**To claim your bonuses and resources, visit
AGamePoker.com/resources**

TABLE OF CONTENTS

Foreword 1
By Phil Galfond
Preface 7
About This Book.. 15
PART 1 19
A-Game Poker
    Chapter 1 21
        Introduction
    Chapter 2 25
        The Evolution of a Winning Poker Player
    Chapter 3 35
        Your Next Big Breakthrough
    Chapter 4 37
        The Mindset Myth
    Chapter 5 39
        The Six Levers of Poker Profits
    Chapter 6 53
        Introducing A-Game Poker
PART 2 59
The Anatomy of an A-Game Player
    Chapter 7 61
        Building An A-Game Player
    Chapter 8 63
        Poker As a Professional Sport
    Pro Case Study 67
        Kevin Martin
        2022 Streamer Of The Year
    Chapter 9 71
        Off the Table Optimization
    Chapter 10 85
        A-Game Skill Stack
    Chapter 11 91
        In-Game Execution
    Pro Case Study 96
        BERRI SWEET
        #1 Heads-Up Player In The World
    Chapter 12 101
        From Knowledge To Action

PART 3 103
Becoming an A-Game Player
    Chapter 13 105
      The A-Game Engine
    Chapter 14 111
      The Power of Vision
    Chapter 15 117
      Scheduling for Success
    Chapter 16 125
      Fuel For High-Performance Poker
    Chapter 17 129
      Excellence Through Exercise
    Chapter 18 133
      Scaling Your Skills
    Chapter 19 143
      The Performance Phase
    Pro Case Study 145
      Brian Rast
      2023 Poker Hall Of Fame Inductee with Over $25,000,000 In Live
      Tournament Earnings
    Chapter 20 147
      The A.G.A.M.E. Pre-Session Protocol
    Chapter 21 155
      The A-Game Audit
    Chapter 22 163
      The Truth About Tilt
    Chapter 23 187
      The Recovery Phase
    Pro Case Study 195
      Kristen Foxen
      Three-Time GPI Female Player of the Year & Four-Time WSOP Bracelet
      Winner
    Chapter 24 199
      Post Session Routine
    Pro Case Study 208
      BenCB
      High-Stakes MTT Professional & Founder of Raise Your Edge
    Chapter 25 211
      Systems For Sleep
    Chapter 26 219
      Recovery Strategies
    Chapter 27 233
      You Know What To Do

PART 4 235
What's Holding You Back?
    Chapter 28 237
      The Four Performance Roadblocks
    Chapter 29 243
      Detrimental Mental Programs
    Chapter 30 249
      Detrimental Mental Program Examples
    Pro Case Study 252
      Phil Galfond
      High-Stakes Professional & Founder of Run It Once Poker
    Pro Case Study 258
      Fedor Holz
      High-Stakes MTT Professional with Over $40,000,000 in Live Earnings
    Pro Case Study 263
      Jon Van Fleet
      High-Stakes MTT Professional with Over $22,000,000 in Online Earnings
    Pro Case Study 274
      Jason Koon
      High-Stakes Professional with Over $52,000,000 in Live Earnings
    Chapter 31 279
      Pulling Back The Curtain
    Pro Case Study 285
      Matt Berkey
      High-Stakes Cash Game Professional & Founder of Solve For Why
    Chapter 32 289
      Dealing With Downswings
    Pro Case Study 296
      Alex Foxen
      High-Stakes MTT Professional with Over $30,000,000 in Live Earnings
    Chapter 33 299
      Lack Of Motivation
Your Next Step 311
    Pro Case Study 313
      Lara Eisenberg
      World Series of Poker Bracelet Winner
Acknowledgments 319
About the Authors..323

FOREWORD

BY PHIL GALFOND

Your outcomes aren't a direct result of your knowledge and skills. They come from your knowledge and skills multiplied by your performance.

As someone who's spent half my life making quick, complex decisions while playing against the best poker players in the world, this was painfully obvious to me from the beginning. At some moments, or even some days, my mind worked on an entirely different level than others. Though I was absolutely aware of these moments as they were occurring, I couldn't predict them or make them happen.

After working in the business world, I realized that the difference between an A-day and a C-day wasn't quite as obvious to me there. I wasn't sure how much it mattered in a more "normal" setting, away from intense competition. That was before I met Elliot Roe and he showed me how I could bring the things he taught not only into my approach to poker but into my approach to my life away from poker.

I've learned the concepts in this book over the years, both through Elliot's course and through working with him directly. Dollar for dollar, I've invested more in Elliot's teachings than in every book I've ever owned or ever will own, but the return on that investment has been enormous. Through some of the concepts and exercises outlined here within, I unlocked potential that would have gone unrealized. I learned to perform well more consistently in all areas of my life. I gained clarity on my life's direction, and I achieved great things by facing fears I wasn't even aware I had.

Let me give you just one of the many examples.

Washed Up?

For over a decade, I had competed in the highest-stakes poker games online against the best players in the world with great success. Then came 2015, when I stepped away from poker to work on my businesses. It was around this time that poker solvers began having a profound impact on the way people played. I had never studied with them before stepping away from the game, and I didn't touch them over the next four years, as I worked on running my businesses.

Truth be told, I was unhappy about solvers. I'd figured out how to beat the biggest games without tools telling me how to play. That was my strength. I was a figure-outer.

Know what I wasn't? A studier. A memorizer. My memory isn't anything to write home about, and I squeaked by without doing my homework in high school by figuring things out during tests. I expected that, in the post-solver era of poker, the winners would no longer be the figure-outers but the studiers. And so, though I never accepted it, I worried that my days as an elite poker player – one who could beat world-class players – were behind me.

That thought, anytime I faced it, made me sad. Poker was the place where I achieved greatness. I played a game that millions played, and I rose to the top. I wasn't ready for that part of my identity – that achievement – to be over.

My whole life, I was told that I could achieve anything I set my mind to, and I believed it. In fact, I made sure not to work too hard so that I could always continue believing it. Elliot calls this the "Too smart to try" program. He taught me how and why it had been installed early in my life and was still running into adulthood.

(I have no doubt that 12-year-old Phil would've been an incredible student if he'd had the opportunity to work with Elliot.)

Through exercises contained in this book, I realized that I was afraid to try to learn from solvers. If I didn't try, I'd never know whether or not I could be a great player again. If I gave it a shot, I might learn that I wasn't as smart as I was told throughout my childhood.

The Galfond Challenge

The exercise continued to help me overcome the fear I'd unearthed, and through further work with Elliot, I devised a plan to help grow my business while doing what I truly loved: Challenging myself against the top players of today. This is how the Galfond Challenge came into being.

I studied with and learned from solvers. I competed on a huge stage, one on one, against world-class players. This was just about the most extreme version of my fear I could dream up, and I faced it, brimming with excitement.

During the first of five challenges, I immediately faced incredible adversity and crushing losses. Thanks to my work with Elliot, I kept my composure and competed admirably.

Through the Galfond Challenges, I learned that I was capable of contending with the best in the post-solver era. I learned that this part of my life didn't have to be over. I simply had to adapt. Competing on the same level with great players would have been enough, but as it turns out, I went on to win all five of my matches! It has been, hands-down, the most rewarding experience of my poker career. I now know with complete confidence that I'll always be able to compete at the poker table if I set my mind to it, and it's hard to express how happy that has made me. Without Elliot, I might have stayed retired. I might have never learned what I was capable of.

You

Perhaps the fears you will uncover will come from someplace else. Maybe the issues holding back your performance are entirely different. Fortunately for you, Elliot has worked with a substantial number of high-performers from all walks of life, helping them navigate their unique sets of goals and challenges. Whatever you want to accomplish and whatever you're dealing with, he's seen it. And – judging by the unanimous glowing reviews from those I've referred to him – he's probably helped conquer it.

As a client of Elliot's, I've long wondered what makes him so good at helping others unlock their greatness. Yes, he's got that experience. Obviously, he's an intelligent problem-solver. Sure, he's had training. But those things are true of other people, too. What is it that sets Elliot Roe apart? It wasn't until I became his friend that I understood.

Elliot is so good at what he does because, save for spending time with family, there is nothing in the world he'd rather be doing than helping others become the best version of themselves. This unmatched passion and dedication are what have shaped him into the master that he is today.

ROI

The contents of this book will lead you to outcomes that may range from small improvements in your performance to huge upgrades in your life as a whole. We're all unique. I don't know which sections of this book will make the difference for you. I just know that some of them will. Think of the work that you do.

What would a 25% increase in your output or performance mean for you?

What would even a 5% increase be worth over the next ten years?

I don't know you, but I can guarantee you'll see a return on the modest investment into this book and the time it will take to put Elliot's wisdom into action. Study this book with the aim of improving your performance in your career, but don't be surprised when something more profound happens.

PREFACE

It's November 2002.

I'm 21 years old and competing in a KSBO Amateur MMA tournament. The tournament is held in a small sports hall in Nottingham, England. It's a simple set up of wrestling mats on the floor and a small section of bleachers for the few spectators who are here to watch. I've been training in kick-boxing since I was 15 or 16 and MMA for the past two years. I've competed in a handful of tournaments previously, and this one starts off just like all the rest.

My heart is racing, I'm full of anxious energy, and my nerves are on edge all before I've even finished my warm up. After what seems to be an eternity, my name is finally called for my first match. My opponent is Paul Daley, who will later go on to fight in the UFC, Strikeforce, and Bellator MMA.

The bell rings and Paul comes forward, throwing punches and kicks. He connects frequently and has me on the backfoot. I manage to tie him up, but he quickly separates, coming right back at me, landing shot after shot. I'm under pressure and finally manage to land a solid left hand to the body. Paul reacts by shooting for a takedown. As he does I manage to sink in a guillotine choke.

It's tight. As we land on the floor I use my momentum to sweep to mount, still holding the choke. He fights for a moment, but the choke is too tight. He taps and I've won my first match.

With 45 minutes to go until my next match, I know I need to relax. I find a quiet spot, but my body still thinks I'm in the fight, and no matter what I try I'm not able to use my mind to convince it otherwise. My heart is racing. I can feel my energy burning away as the clock counts down to the start of my second match.

Stepping onto the mat for my second match, I already feel exhausted. The bell rings. I immediately shoot for a takedown and land it. I'm on top, in his guard, consistently landing strikes. I'm in the dominant position, winning the round, but with every strike that I throw I feel my energy depleting. With a minute and a half to go in the round, I'm totally exhausted, so drained that in the dying seconds, I allow my opponent to land a Hail Mary armbar.

With more energy I could have fought it off. He didn't have great position and the attempt wasn't very tight, but my gas tank was empty. All I needed to do to win the fight was to hold on for a few more seconds. Even so, I knew that I'd used up so much energy that I had little chance of winning my next match. So, instead of fighting on, I tapped and was out of the tournament.

After this experience, I continued training for a few more years but injuries prevented me from ever competing seriously again. Fighters like Paul Daley, Michael Bisping, and Dan Hardy all got their start in that very same organization, and I came to realize that even if I had the physical skills to compete with them, at that time in my life I didn't have what it took mentally to succeed at a higher level.

I didn't know it at the time, but this was a turning point in my life. I knew exactly what it felt like to fall short in a big moment, and that became the catalyst of my journey to help others succeed.

However, my transformation didn't come about immediately. After I left the amateur MMA scene, I went on to work a conventional career in real estate and renewable energy investments. In fact, my reintroduction to the high-performance world was a bit of a fluke.

I'd always had a fear of flying, which was affecting me in my career and interfering with my ability to travel anywhere for a holiday. I could manage getting *on* a plane, but I was a nervous wreck for the week leading up to the flight and, once I reached my destination, immediately began ruminating about the return flight home.

After witnessing my fear of flying, a good friend of mine suggested that I try hypnotherapy to resolve it. Though I trusted my friend enough to give it a try, I went into my hypnotherapy session fully convinced that it wouldn't work.

What happened next caught me completely off guard.

During my in-person session (this was well before the days of Zoom), my hypnotherapist had me lay down on a couch, close my eyes, and relax. After guiding me to a place of deep relaxation, she asked me to recall the last time I'd been on a flight and to describe the feelings and sensations I felt in my body at that moment. As soon as I was fully immersed in those sensations, she asked me to jump back to the very first time I could remember feeling that way.

Suddenly, I found myself recalling a memory that until that very moment I'd forgotten. I'm a small child, at my grandfather's house, looking at a photograph on the wall of a small plane. My mum is telling me about an accident that has just happened: the plane used by my grandfather's business crashed, killing his business partner. As I said, this wasn't something that I was even sure about, it just sort of bubbled up, and I had to later confirm the story with my mum to be sure that it had actually happened.

As I was experiencing the memory in the moment, the hypnotherapist suggested I look at the situation from my adult perspective, injecting the logic that just because someone I knew had died in a plane crash, it didn't mean that flying was significantly more dangerous for me, especially when it came to long-haul commercial flights.

It's hard to describe the way I felt when I walked out of her office–the closest I can get is that I felt like a weight had been lifted and replaced with a sensation of lightness. I knew at that moment that the next time I got on a plane, I would no longer be consumed by worries or fear. I had walked into that hypnotherapy session terrified to fly. When I walked out, the fear was gone.

Yet I was the same person. Nothing about *me* had changed. Fear of flying was simply a program I was running in the background; I wasn't even aware of it. And I had just discovered that it was possible to rewrite that program, to rewrite that memory from when I was a child in a way that benefitted me.

As amazed and happy as I was to have conquered my fear of flying, as I stepped out into the street, all I could think about was just how powerful the mind truly is and just how much is possible when we become aware of the programs we're running and take back control. I connected back to that moment in the MMA tournament. I'd always known that it had been my inability to control my fear that had caused me to burn through all my energy and had led to me to quit from exhaustion.

I now understood that if I could help others overcome their fears in high-pressure moments, I could dramatically tip the table in their favor. I was no longer thinking about my next flight, all I could think about was how much better the world would be if we removed our roadblocks and were able to perform up to our full potential.

After that experience, I quickly enrolled in the top hypnotherapy school I could find, and after receiving my certification, I hired many of the top experts and authors in the field to continue my training directly.

After testing the water with friends and family, I started taking on clients, including some golfers. I was introduced to poker through a friend in the industry. She said if my methods worked well with golfers, they could have a huge impact on poker players.

This was in the early 2010s. With my poker clients it quickly became apparent that their profitability could be dramatically improved if they adopted my mindset coaching techniques to help them overcome self-sabotage, fear of failure, and fear of success. Since the best poker players are always looking for new ways to gain an edge, word spread quickly throughout the industry.

The majority of my work throughout the first 10 years of my career has been working with professional poker players, and having the opportunity to work with the best of the best, I've been able to use the game as a foundation for developing and iterating the mindset and performance coaching strategies I now use on a daily basis with my clients.

Poker is one of the most robust environments when it comes to mental performance. To be successful at the game you must be resilient, determined, curious, and able to think in a way that is almost completely opposite of how your brain tends to operate naturally. Beyond poker, I've had the opportunity to work with UFC Champions, Olympic medalists, CEOs, and Wall Street traders, and I can honestly say that without the work I've done with poker players, I wouldn't be the coach I am today.

Just like my clients, my career has continued to evolve. The majority of my work these days is with company founders, CEOs, large hedge fund managers, and those who have recently completed large company exits. To be clear, I still work with poker players, but it's no longer feasible for me to work directly with any but the top players and those playing in the biggest games out there.

Nevertheless, I am still very involved and active in the poker world. I created the Primed Mind app, which includes an entire section dedicated to poker players. I created the A-Game Poker Masterclass, which is my flagship poker training product. It walks you through my complete A-Game Poker system, with action plans and exercises designed to take you from learning to implementation. I've trained a team of coaches in my methodology, and now have coaches at investment levels that make sense at all levels of the game.

You can learn more about these additional resources by visiting: AGamePoker.com/resources

This book is the final piece of the puzzle when it comes to creating a full suite of poker mindset & performance tools and training. My goal is to make sure that anyone who wants to become successful at the game, and is willing to do what it takes to get there, won't fall short because of a lack of knowledge. With this book, and the A-Game Poker Masterclass, I've laid out everything I know about achieving success in this game and how to implement the tools I describe into your game.

Whether this is your first introduction to my content or you've been following me for years, I think you'll find this book invaluable. Beyond the game itself, this book is about creating the life you desire—and that's not a topic you study once and are done with.

So, wherever you are on your journey, I appreciate you having me along for the ride.

ABOUT THIS BOOK

I am not a doctor, researcher, psychologist or mental health professional. This is not an academic book. This is not peer-reviewed research, nor will I spend much time discussing the underlying mechanisms and scientific studies backing up the strategies I share herein. I have huge admiration and respect for those who do that type of work and write those types of books. It's important work, just not the type of work I do.

I am a performance coach, working with clients to directly transform their results. This book is the culmination of over 10,000 hours of working one-on-one with professional poker players and seeing what works and what doesn't when helping them reach the highest levels of success. My clients put millions of dollars on the line each year, and a large majority of them become significantly more profitable after working with me than they were when we started.

My poker clients have cashed for over $250,000,000 in tournaments and won virtually every major title in the game, including the WSOP Main Event, The Super High Roller Bowl, One Drop, the WCOOP Main Event, as well as winning many WSOP, WCOOP and SCOOP events. My high-stakes cash-game clients tend to prefer to remain anonymous, and I only like to share results that are verifiable, so let's just say the amount of money my clients have won in cash games is significant. In the heads-up arena, I've now helped multiple clients win large public and private heads-up challenges in dominating fashion.

This book shows the systems used by the world's top players to gain an edge over their competition. It provides the framework for becoming a "professional" poker player. And I don't mean that in the sense of playing the game as your only source of income. A full-time player can treat the game like an amateur just as easily as a part-time player can approach it with high levels of professionalism.

Poker is a choice. You can choose to treat the game as a professional sport and embrace the opportunity to get paid like a professional athlete or choose to treat it like a game and be lucky to break even.

This book is written for those who want to maximize their profits, understanding that to have better results than others you must do what they are not willing to do. The majority of the money in poker is made by the top one percent of players. This book will show you what it takes to join that top percent.

There will be sections of this book where you may feel triggered. You may notice where you're holding yourself back from the life you want to lead. This book will not only show you a framework but will dig deeper, showing you the subconscious programs you and many poker players struggle with when working through the game.

Some of my most successful clients have been kind enough to share their stories of overcoming their detrimental mental programs on their path to the top. While some of these stories may not hit a nerve with you, others will undoubtedly resonate, and you may discover that you're struggling with the exact same issues that some of my clients have faced. Use their stories to gain an understanding of your own programs and triggers so you can begin the work of personal exploration needed to better understand yourself and your own issues. We have a team of coaches available if you're looking to explore further.

Ryan Carter, co-author of this book has been my business partner for the last 10 years. He has worked with me to create the strategies my clients have used over the last decade and translate my ideas into actionable content that goes beyond my 1:1 sessions.

I'd like to thank all of my clients, those directly involved in the book and those I've worked with over the years who have helped develop and field test the concepts and strategies you'll find in these pages. Without them none of this would be possible.

PART 1

Competing at the highest level of poker requires focus and mental toughness. Without Elliot's help, I wouldn't have been able to become the #1 ranked poker player in the world. I look forward to continuing working with Elliot as I attempt to match, or surpass, that success in other ventures.

- Fedor Holz - High-Stakes MTT Professional with Over $40,000,000 in Live Earnings

CHAPTER 1

INTRODUCTION

Mindset.

It's a word that elicits a wide range of emotions within the poker community. Some hear the word and think of the self-deluded players who believe that positive thoughts can substitute for strategic skills and tactical execution. Others hear the word and are certain it's a critical component of the well-rounded skill set of the biggest winners in the modern poker era.

What is the actual value of mindset in relation to success in poker? While I have no illusions that I'll be able to persuade all the hardcore skeptics, my goal with this book is to convince those of you who are open minded. If I do my job well, you'll come to see that mindset is essential for anyone who wants to be a long-term winner.

I don't expect you to be free of skepticism. In fact, healthy skepticism is an attribute that nearly all top poker players have in common. If anyone understands the skeptical mind of a poker player, it's me. I got my start in the poker world over a decade ago by convincing professional poker players that hypnosis was an effective tool to improve their results at the table. A-Game Poker is my attempt to distill into a system everything I've learned in my decade-plus of working with poker players. I think all but the most skeptical among you will be able to embrace it.

My ask is this: If you read this book and are convinced of the value of working on this area of your game, please take action on what you've learned. My passion for coaching comes from the energy I get from seeing the success of the players I've worked with and hearing their stories. I'll share some of those stories in the pages of this book. I would love for you to be the next story. To be someone who uses what you'll discover in this book to achieve your most ambitious goals in the game.

Who Is A-Game Poker For?

A-Game Poker is for anyone who wants to optimize their long-term success in poker and is willing to put in the work necessary to do so. The saying, "Poker is a hard way to make an easy living," has never been more true. If you're hoping that this book will reveal "secret mindset techniques and hacks" that will allow you to skip the hard work of building a strong technical game, this book is not for you. If you're looking at poker as an easy way to get rich quickly, this book is not for you. If you expect to read this book and instantly become a poker crusher, this book is not for you.

To be successful in this game you need a system for developing and expanding your technical skills at a rate that outpaces your competition. You also need to consistently apply those skills at the table. A-Game Poker is for anyone who wants to learn how the best players in the world are doing that.

How To Use This Book

This book is broken up into four main parts.

In Part 1, I'll show you the evolution of a winning poker player, share my definition of A-Game poker, and show you why implementing the core principles is essential for long-term success in the game.

In Part 2, I'll break down the Anatomy of an A-Game Player and reveal the key systems, mental models, and strategies that the best players in the world apply.

In Part 3, I'll share some of my most powerful systems and strategies, so you can quickly go from the theoretical to the practical.

In Part 4, we'll uncover the barriers and roadblocks that are currently preventing you from implementing A-Game Poker in your game.

You will get the most value from this book by reading it in chronological order and completing any action steps before moving on. You may be tempted to skip around to the topics that seem most relevant to you now, but I strongly advise you to read this book in the order it was written. If you start with the "What" and the "How" before understanding the "Why," you'll find the strategies I lay out much less effective.

Chapter 2

The Evolution of a Winning Poker Player

Sometimes, to understand where we are going we must first understand where we've been.

In most professional sports, there are fierce debates about who's the GOAT (greatest of all time).

Wilt Chamberlain. Michael Jordan. Kobe Bryant. Lebron James.

Babe Ruth. Hank Aaron. Barry Bonds. Mike Trout.

Pelé. Diego Maradona. Lionel Messi. Cristiano Ronaldo.

Some contend that, if transported into the present, the greats of old would still dominate in the modern era, while others are firm in the view that the new breed of athlete would obliterate the oldtimers.

In poker, there isn't much debate. If we were to break the game down into distinct eras and pluck out the top players from each, the modern players would wipe the table and empty the bank accounts of the older generation. The game of poker is, in fact, a fascinating study of performance evolution. Pluck an online crusher from the early 2000s and put him in a small stakes online game today and he'd get destroyed.

The obvious caveat is that mental performance competitions are different from physical ones, so older generation players have the ability to evolve their skillsets over a larger time horizon. Which is to say, that online crusher we transported through time would certainly start out a loser in a game today, but if they followed the strategies of this book, they'd certainly have the opportunity to improve. The point is that in poker, what it took to win a year ago, is different than what it takes to win today, and that's even more true when you look back five, ten or even fifty years into the past.

One of the techniques I use as a mindset & performance coach is visualization. This is where I get the client in a very relaxed state and have them picture scenarios and outcomes we want to work on. Usually in these situations, the client will have their eyes closed so they can put all their focus on creating mental imagery. It's not as potent while reading a book, but we can access some of these same pathways by having you read text written in a highly visual manner.

Ready?

We're about to take you on a journey through the history of poker to discover what it once took to be the best in the world.

Take a few deep breaths with me now.

Breathe in…out…in….out…

Imagine we're in a time machine, traveling back to the Texas road gambler days…this is where the legend of Doyle Brunson began, where he and his fellow road gamblers were among the first to make poker their primary livelihood and source of income.

In this vision, we're transported to the smoke-filled back room of a laundromat. A group of men sit around a poker table. Some of them are gruff and gritty, their rough hands the hands of laborers, oil riggers, ranch hands, auto mechanics. Others are well-dressed businessmen, lawyers, and salesmen.

The game is no-limit Texas hold'em.

As we watch them play, we notice that they're all pretty much ABC players in terms of strategy: they raise when they have a good starting hand, bet the flop when they hit it, and check when they miss. Check-raising in these games is actually frowned upon, considered ungentlemanly, even underhanded.

Enter Doyle Brunson, who dominates games like these by moving from what is essentially a "face up" style to a more aggressive approach that exploits the general passiveness of his opponents.

He raises mediocre hands in position. He makes continuation bets on most flops. He bluffs, regularly making big raises with draws. Actions that are standard even from the weakest players today make him a legend in these games.

Taking a few more deep breaths, we are now transported a few decades beyond the young Doyle and Texas to mid-90's Atlantic City.

Limit games, particularly 7-card stud, dominate the cardrooms, but you can also find the occasional no limit hold'em game spread at some private tables in the city or at the famed Mayfair Club in Gramercy Park–and of course there's the Main Event of the World Series of Poker at Binion's Horseshoe in Las Vegas, which is played as no-limit hold'em.

The shift from the road gambler days are incremental. Other than a few anomalies, most of the top players are in their 40s and 50s, as it takes years to learn and refine your game.

Now, let's flash forward to 2003.

You see a player at their computer, playing on PokerStars.

In the background, a TV tuned to ESPN shows some guy named Chris Moneymaker playing heads up against Sammy

Farha for the Main Event title. A whole new generation of mostly college age kids is swept up by the excitement of seeing players' hole cards, visible through the magic of hole-card cameras; it's captivating to be able to follow the decision-making process of the top players. And online poker, in its infancy, gives them a unique opportunity to practice and explore the game for themselves.

Watching the televised championship, it's evident that a solid, straightforward style is very much getting the job done. Players stick to a tight opening range and look to extract maximum value when they hit a good hand. They bet for value on three streets with weak, top-pair hands. They're excited to get it all in on the flop with top-pair-top kicker knowing their opponents will have a hard time letting even weak one-pair hands go.

In this era, players looking to improve their games have little to work with. Some foundational strategy books such as Super System and The Theory Of Poker are available, and online message boards and forums are starting to emerge, but at this point poker is still very much a game that is learned from experience and internal processing.

And, with that, the year is 2006.

The game has absolutely exploded in popularity since our last stop in the timeline. Televised poker is a legitimate sensation, fully fueled by the advertising dollars of the online poker sites who are taking full advantage of the online poker boom. The best poker players are now legitimate B-list celebrities. Players who grinded out a living on the live circuit are thrust into the limelight. Televised poker needs its cast of heroes and villains. As the online high-stakes scene forms, legends are born. For the first time in history, you can watch players battle, with hundreds of thousands of dollars on the line each hand.

While by no means a conventional occupation, becoming a professional poker player is something that no longer seems accessible only to a select few. Playing the game for a living has transcended its seedy hustler past, becoming a reasonable choice for college students to opt for (or at least attempt) over a career in one of the more traditional professions.

At this time, everything poker is in high demand. Along with online poker, televised games, packed cardrooms, there's more poker content being created than at any time in the history of the game. Player-tracking websites, database software, and video training sites all contribute to a quantum leap in player skill acquisition.

Online players are now able to replay their hands, study their mistakes, and discover areas of the game in which their opponents are weak. Video training sites give some of the best poker teachers in the world the opportunity to offer a "peek over my shoulder" experience, and teach lessons as the game evolves in real time.

We're now in 2012.

The glimmer and shine that was present at our last stop has started to fade. Poker has had a rough go of it lately, with the US Government essentially banning online poker in the US on April 15th, 2011, a date otherwise known as Black Friday. US professionals who want to continue playing online are forced to leave the country, and the largest segment of the worldwide player pool is removed in the blink of an eye.

At first, many people declare the game dead. There's just no way that poker can survive without the US market. However, you'll notice that the savvy player you're watching sees this as an opportunity. They get a crew together to rent a house in Mexico, finding that the post-Black Friday games are actually quite lucrative.

While the US market was huge, many of the pros are Americans, and very few of them have taken quick action to relocate. Players who thrive in this era do so not because they're employing any major strategic breakthroughs but because, instead of wallowing in this changed reality, they're taking advantage of the opportunity that the new landscape presents. Instead of bellyaching and saying, "There's no way I can move to another country," they continue to study the game, branch out, reconfigure their lives and stay in action. They survive this hard time, continuing to grow while many others simply give up.

Now we're in 2017.

The poker world has found its footing once again. While the total market is smaller than during the boom, it seems that no matter what happens there will always be people who want to play poker.

The big shift in skill acquisition is the accessibility and popularization of GTO solvers. With a skilled user and enough computing power you're now able to discover the game theory optimal solution for many situations.

This begins to shift the type of player best suited for success. Even with all the previous study tools available, it was the player who could internally synthesize that input and translate it to the table who proved to be most successful. Now, the players able to make the fastest leap in skill are the ones who study hardest, are the best at memorization and have the ability to ask the programs the right questions.

Training sites are still in high demand, particularly the ones with the coaches and trainers most capable of disseminating these strategies. We also see a rise in comprehensive and highly structured courses compared to the scattershot approach most training sites have taken in the past.

Now, we're in 2023.

You find yourself in Las Vegas near the end of the WSOP. Registration for the Main Event has closed with a record breaking 10,043 entrants. They've just announced a first-place prize of $12.1 million. There's a feeling in the air that we're at the beginning of a new poker boom.

Beyond a growing momentum in the United States for legalized online poker, high-stakes live streams are filling the role that televised tournaments served during the first poker boom, and there has been a significant uptick in interest for poker content of all kinds.

With that momentum comes training resources that make the most advanced strategies and understanding of the game available to anyone with a desire to access them. Solvers are no longer a tool that require a PhD in mathematics and a farm of servers to run; they're able to give results in real time and use artificial intelligence to guide the training in a more optimal way. The training sites have further refined their content to share training from the best players in the world in formats that make difficult concepts easy to understand. The tools are so advanced and sophisticated that the greatest risk to the game at the moment is how to prevent players from using them in real time while playing.

Most of the top players in this ever more competitive atmosphere have moved beyond focusing purely on technical skill acquisition into understanding the need for overall performance optimization. Final tables that were once filled with out-of-shape junk-food eaters, are now the domain of players who look like highly-tuned athletes.

Being a successful player in this era is certainly lucrative, but the competition is fierce and getting fiercer. As you contemplate the evolution of poker that we've seen on our little journey through time and consider the change and growth yet to come, take a breath with me… and let us come back to the present moment.

I have no way to know when you'll be reading this book, and no way to be certain how poker will evolve from here. What I do know is that it will evolve, that the game is fluid and resilient. In all of the eras that we visited during this exercise, there were plenty of people predicting the game's demise.

I've written this book to be an evergreen resource for poker players who want to dominate the modern poker game, whatever direction it may take in the future. Obviously if poker is a main source of income for you, then you should pay close attention to the macro economy of the game, to understand if continuing to play aligns with your overall vision.

What I can tell you with certainty is this:

As poker continues to evolve, the players who will be most successful are the ones who evolve with it most quickly. Transport to today a player who crushed decades ago, and they wouldn't stand a chance in the modern game. Undoubtedly, they'll say the same thing about players from today, ten, twenty or a hundred years from now.

The goal of this book is to give you the tools you'll need to be a player who evolves with the game, rather than a player who gets left behind. Because, make no mistake, if you do not acquire those tools, you *will* get left behind. There are more formerly elite players who are no longer able to keep up with the modern environment than there are those who have made it to the top and been able to maintain their position.

If there is a new poker boom on the horizon, do you want to be the player already in position to take advantage of it, or the player scrambling to play catch up?

CHAPTER 3

YOUR NEXT BIG BREAKTHROUGH

The more the strategic game of poker evolves the more you need to look for additional edges in less obvious facets of the game.

The Texas road gamblers, led by Doyle Brunson, could dominate their games simply by making continuation bets and semi-bluffs. The early Vegas/Atlantic City grinders could dominate their games with good hand selection and basic aggression. The first wave of online poker pros took things to the next level with in-position 3-bets and multi-street bluffs. The Post-Black Friday crushers introduced GTO strategies and solver-based study. Today's modern game has all the hard-won knowledge garnered by previous generations, plus near real-time GTO solvers and AI powered trainers.

In a poker era where access to information is not a limiting factor and the game has evolved to the point where it is harder than ever to find massive strategic advantages, how do you create an edge? Is it possible that poker has been solved? Is it on the verge of becoming unprofitable?

I'm here to tell you that for as long as there has been poker there has been someone saying that the game is dead. I'm also here to tell you that the next big breakthrough is not strategic. In fact, the next big breakthrough involves a physical and mental approach to the game, revolving around what I call the Fundamental Performance Question, which is the foundation of everything I do as a coach.

The Fundamental Performance Question

The Fundamental Performance Question is very simple:

"What are the best players in the world doing to be successful that I am not?"

To be successful in any area of life, there are three crucially related questions you need to ask yourself: What are the best in the world doing? What am I doing? And what is the gap between the two?

What I do to help my clients achieve the success they desire, not only in poker but in sports and business, is to first identify the gap, and then advise them on the actions needed to close it. Simple in concept, not simple in execution.

In previous poker eras, the most significant element of this gap was a technical one. The difference between the best players in the world and those struggling to break even was access to strategies and knowledge that the latter didn't have. In the evolution of the game, that gap has narrowed to a point where what separates the biggest winners in the world and low stakes grinders, at least from a strategic standpoint, has never been smaller.

That's why your next big breakthrough will not be a strategic one. The goal of this book is to give you the knowledge you need to answer the Fundamental Performance Question for your own poker game and get you started in closing the distance between you and the top players in the world.

CHAPTER 4

THE MINDSET MYTH

I want to make one thing clear when exploring the Fundamental Performance Question in a poker context. Just because the number of strategic breakthroughs that remain are limited, that doesn't mean I'm advocating you ignore this area. Far from it.

A deep and current knowledge of the strategic game is absolutely essential if you want to be a significant winner over the long term in poker's highest echelons. But it's no longer enough by itself, not even in the mid-stakes games. It means that using the best tools available to deepen your strategic knowledge, while necessary, is not sufficient to beat the game at mid to high stakes.

If poker were a hot Vegas night club, elite knowledge of the game gets you on the list but doesn't guarantee access to the VIP section.

Beyond their firm grasp of the strategic game, what are the best poker players in the world doing that you aren't? This is where you probably expect me to start talking about "The Mental Game of Poker" or "Poker Mindset." Even though I label myself a "Mindset and Performance Coach" I actually dislike the term "mindset," because for all intents and purposes, poker, like chess, is a game entirely of the mind and so the terms "mindset" and "mental game" can lead to confusion and lack of clarity in terms of their meaning.

For example, you're playing an MTT and find yourself on the button with Ah4h with 75-blind effective stacks and a raise and a call in front of you—is your decision to 3-bet a "mental game" decision or a strategic decision?

Or say you're playing a deep stack cash game and find yourself with a missed flush draw after check-raising the flop and firing the turn—is the decision to bluff 100bb on the river a "mental game" decision or a strategic decision?

Most people would say these are strategic decisions, but all the processing and decision making is happening in your mind, making the distinction between mental and strategic less than obvious.

A hypothetical: If you were to ask 100 serious poker players what having a "strong mental game" meant, what do you think they would say? How would you answer this question? In my experience, 90 out of 100 would say that having a strong mental game means not tilting at the tables. The ten who actually understand that a strong mental game encompasses much more than that? Well, they would be students of my A-Game Poker Masterclass.

I developed the concept of A-Game Poker to give players a clear understanding of all the elements that go into developing a world-class poker game. To be able to accurately answer the fundamental question, "What are the best players in the world doing that I'm not?" It's necessary to first understand all the possible ways you can gain an edge in the game.

CHAPTER 5

THE SIX LEVERS OF POKER PROFITS

Technical skill, as I said before and want to emphasize again, is the foundation for any successful poker player. It is a misconception many players have about my work as a mindset coach that I steer players away from working on their technical skills and direct them to put more emphasis on other areas. In fact, nothing could be further from the truth. The truth is that during my earliest years of coaching, I spent a good deal of my time working to convince my clients that they needed to devote more time to working on their technical game. This might be hard to believe, but even in the Post-Black Friday era, many of the best players thought they knew everything about the game and didn't need to spend any time studying.

In today's games anyone who's serious about beating any but the smallest stakes games likely does most if not all of the following:

- Subscribes to multiple training sites
- Participates in group coaching or is in an active study group
- Works with a 1:1 coach
- Uses solver-based study tools

Every year dozens of books are released. Every month hundreds of hours of video training are created. Massively powerful software programs are available for a nominal price. And many of the game's elite are sharing their best strategies with their private coaching clients. Why then, with so much great poker content being produced, do so many players struggle to achieve the success they desire? The simple answer? Information alone isn't enough to get you where you want to be. Poker skill, while obviously incredibly important to your success, is only one piece of the puzzle.

What I've discovered is that it's one of the six major elements that determine your profitability in the game. If you're not having the success you desire, then it's at least one of six factors that's holding you back. Before I dive into what the factors are, I'm going to run through a quick visualization that will serve as an introduction to the topic.

As you read through this next section, spend some time creating a mental picture of the scenario I describe. Feel free to stop reading and close your eyes for a moment if that helps make the visualization more powerful. Try to make the image as real as possible.

Ready?

The Control Room

Imagine you're in a large control room.

This control room is your mind, and it regulates your thoughts, emotions, and actions.

As you're looking around you notice a door, and above it, a sign that reads "Poker Profits." You open the door to find a dimly lit room and a large lever labeled "Poker Skill." Next to the lever is a digital display that shows "Expected Profits Next 12 Months."

You grab hold of the lever and start to raise it. At first it lifts relatively easily, and you see your "Expected Profits" number rising at a similar pace. The more you lift it, though, the harder it gets. You also notice that the "Expected Profits" number is only going up a fraction of the amount it was before. You keep trying with all your strength to get that number to go higher, but your "Expected Profit" number won't budge another inch. You push and push and push with all your might, but no matter how hard you try, that "Expected Profit" number just won't move.

Eventually you give up and slump back against the wall. As you sit there, trying to catch your breath, you notice a light switch. You stand up and flick it on to reveal that the room is much larger than you originally realized. Along the wall next to "Poker Skill" are five additional levers, six in total. You get up and start adjusting them, and notice that as you manipulate these new levers, your "Expected Profit" number changes. You notice that adjusting some of the levers affects the others, some positively and some negatively. You're not quite sure of the perfect combination just yet, but you feel a sense of relief knowing that there is more than just the Poker Skill lever that affects your profits, and that all of these factors are under your control.

All right, now take a moment…

Have you ever felt what I just described when trying to raise the level of your game? That no matter how much time and effort you're putting into it, the needle isn't moving? Sadly, this is an all-too-common experience. The good news is that you've been focusing your attention too narrowly and by expanding your frame of reference to include the other available levers, you can and will increase your profitability.

The six levers I've determined have a direct effect on your results are:

Skill - Your absolute knowledge of the game.

Edge - The gap in skill between you and your opponents.

Efficiency - The percentage of time you apply the full extent of your skill to a hand.

Volume - How often you apply your poker skills for real money.

Stakes - The size of the games you play.

Rake - The fee you are charged by the house to play.

These are the six factors that make up the system that produces your poker profits. They are not independent elements, they are holistic, each one deeply connected and intertwined with the others. This is a crucial thing to understand. When you are dealing with an integrated system, focusing on one area and neglecting others is a recipe for disaster. Raise one lever slightly and your profits go up. Raise the same lever too much and it might cause another to drop, resulting in your overall profits going down. Since these levers are symbiotic, it's impossible to declare one more important than another (or at least it's a valueless exercise to undertake).

The most skilled player in the world who plays against stiff competition (edge), tilts often (efficiency), and rarely plays (volume) will make less money than a mediocre player who plays often (volume) against very weak competition (edge) at very high stakes (stakes).

A good example of this would be Dan Bilzerian. Dan doesn't have the reputation of being an elite player, but he's rumored to have made over $50,000,000 in profits by playing against ultra-rich amateurs in private cash games. So, while you personally may have more skill than Dan, skill isn't an asset you can take to the bank and exchange for cash. The poker player who is most successful is the one who can optimize as many levers as possible in order to maximize their profits.

Let's take a deeper look at each of the six levers I've mentioned and explore how they interact with the other five. When I say a particular lever positively correlates with another specific lever, I mean that raising that lever will likely raise the other. When I say a particular lever negatively correlates with another lever, I mean that raising that lever will likely lower the other. (Note: This is neither a good thing or a bad thing, it is simply a consequence.)

Your "Expected Profit" number is the only thing that matters, so sometimes raising one lever and lowering another will be optimal in that regard. For example, playing in a tougher game but at higher stakes (Raising Stakes and Lowering Edge) will often be more profitable than playing against weaker opponents at lower stakes). When I say a lever is neutral with another it just means that raising or lowering it usually has no effect on the other. Remember, these correlations are general statements and examples. You'll have scenarios and combinations where raising a lever for one person might be a positive for that person but a negative for another.

This isn't about coming up with an exact formula, it's about understanding where your profits come from and how these factors interact with each other. Once you have this understanding, you'll be able to apply it to your game and unique situation.

Skill

The first lever, as we've discussed, is *skill*.

Your skill represents your absolute knowledge of the game. If 0 represents someone who's never heard the word poker before and 100 represents someone who has solved every aspect of the game, it's pretty much a given that your skill-number will fall somewhere in between. Skill is the main area of focus for most dedicated players, and it's why the vast majority of poker training products cater to players looking to raise their skill level.

Not surprisingly, skill positively correlates with all the other levers besides *rake*. If you increase your skill level and your opponents do not (or yours improves at a faster rate), then you will increase your *edge*. Having more skill also gives you a wider selection of lineups to choose from. The best player in the world can sit down in any game and be profitable (pre-rake).

Increasing skill will often increase *efficiency*. The prime example of this is a new player who goes on stone-cold tilt if their aces get cracked. A skilled player has a deeper understanding of how the game works and where profits come from. Thus, they understand that getting their aces cracked is just a standard outcome of variance and are therefore more resilient when it happens.

Confidence is closely tied with skill, which is closely tied with *volume*. Confidence is simply trusting that you have the skills to accomplish a task, which comes from putting in the work to gain those skills. Putting in volume is much easier when you feel confident, thus raising skill, which instills that confidence, can enable or encourage you to raise volume. As mentioned earlier, increasing your skill gives you a wider selection of games to choose from, which in turn makes it easier to put in volume.

As stakes increase, the level of competition usually (but not always) increases alongside it. As skill increases, so too does your ability to be profitable at higher stakes. To be a top earner in the game, beating high stakes is essential, and to do that you need a lot of skill.

So, yes, skill is very important. Still, it is just one part of the overall system that determines your profit. Amongst many poker players there's an ongoing debate about what's more important, *technical training* or *mental game/mindset training* (what I call *A-Game Poker*). The smartest players in the game sidestep this debate entirely, understanding that it's all integrated and that debating the issue is just a waste of time.

Edge

Next up we have *Edge*.

Your edge represents the gap in skill between you and your opponents. The larger the gap the larger your edge, and the bigger your profits become. Hopefully you are starting to see how the different levers interact, and how you can increase your profits even without an increase in skill.

Play in a game with players who are very close to your skill level, and your edge will be small, and so will your profits. Play in the same game with players who have a lesser absolute skill level, and your edge increases, as does your profits. You could be the eighth best player in the world, but if you're playing against numbers one through seven, you rate to be a loser. On the other hand, you could be the eighth worst player in the world, but if you play regularly in a game with the seven who are even worse than you, over the long run you're going to take their money.

Edge positively correlates with *efficiency* and *volume*. The larger your edge (aka your win rate), the fewer swings you'll have, meaning your profits will steadily go up, and you won't experience as much variance as someone playing with a smaller edge. This means you'll face less adversity and have a stronger feeling of control. In such an environment, it's relatively easy to play your best (efficiency) and put in a lot of volume.

There are some scenarios where the opposite could be true. If you're playing with a high edge, but for low stakes, the lack of challenge could lead to boredom and thus a drop in efficiency and volume.

By now, you should be starting to see just how important it is to find the right balance for your game in order to optimize your profit number.

Efficiency

Now we have *efficiency*, a major bottleneck for most players.

You probably know someone who seems to have all the right answers when doing work off the table but is constantly making big mistakes in game. They *should* know better but keep making the same mistakes anyway. These are what are known as unforced errors in the sports world. Efficiency represents the percentage of time you apply the full extent of your absolute skill to a hand. All the skill in the world is irrelevant if you're not actually applying it at the table. When someone is performing at peak efficiency, using the full extent of their poker skills and making their best decisions (regardless of outcome), it is often referred to as playing their "A-Game."

While we will cover all six levers in this book, much of what I teach is focused on making the gap between absolute skill and applied skill as small as possible. An extreme example would be a very good player playing highly intoxicated. The skill is there, but the state of impairment prevents the full application of that skill. Tilt is another reason why you might not be applying your full skill every hand you play. Poor health, lack of focus, and stress, are other factors that reduce your efficiency.

Efficiency positively correlates with edge and volume. When there is a large gap between how well you *can* play, and how well you do play, your edge becomes smaller. Playing significantly below your abilities is incredibly frustrating and a definite motivation killer. So, when efficiency drops, volume usually drops with it. On the other hand, when you're playing at your absolute best, you can gain serious momentum and easily put in extra volume.

Volume

Speaking of *volume*, it's our fourth lever of poker profits.

Volume is simply how often you play for real money: the number of hands you play in cash games or the number of games you play in MTTs and SNGs. Volume is how you translate poker skill into actual profits. As I said with efficiency, all the skill in the world is irrelevant if you're not actually applying it at the table. Simply put: If you don't play, you don't get paid.

Volume is a major leak for many players. You can be highly skilled, play in amazing games, and always play your A-Game, but if you only play a few hours a week your earnings will be capped. Keeping all other factors static, a 25% increase in your volume will yield a 25% increase in profits. That's obtainable for many players who constantly struggle with putting in the hours necessary to achieve their profit targets.

It's a balancing act because volume is usually negatively correlated with efficiency. An online player who adds more tables will eventually start to lower their efficiency. It's just not possible to play each hand optimally with so much action going on at once.

Too much volume can also lead to burnout, which can both lower your efficiency and your volume. Burned-out players often need to take weeks or months off to recover and, in the process, give up any profits they would have earned over that time.

Stakes

Next, we have *stakes*.

The stakes you play have a major impact on your overall profitability potential. Moving up through the ranks increases your lifetime profit potential exponentially but doing it too quickly can set you back months or even years. Managing this balancing act well is a vital skill that can mean the difference between a long and prosperous career and one that never makes it off the ground.

For the most part, the rake lever is independent of the others. However, stakes negatively correlate with rake, meaning the higher the stakes you play, the less rake you usually pay, proportionally. This is especially important at the micro and low stakes, where rake can eat up most of the money in the game.

Stakes are often (but not always) negatively correlated with edge, as the further you move up, the stiffer the competition gets. For a player just moving up or taking a shot at higher stakes, you'll usually find a negative correlation with efficiency. Playing for an amount of money that will really sting if you lose, isn't a great recipe for playing your best poker. On the other hand, a player used to higher stakes might have a lower efficiency when playing smaller stakes if they fail to treat the smaller game as seriously.

Rake

And finally, we have *rake*.

Rake is the least sexy of all the levers, but it's important to be aware of the rake that you're paying and how it affects your overall profitability. A high rake, like you'll often find in micro and low stakes games, can eat up all your profits, while a low rake can make players profitable who would be losers under average circumstances. A good example of that would be the old SuperNova Elite grinders who might, during a losing session, still come out ahead after factoring in rakeback and bonuses.

A high rake also doesn't necessarily mean you need to avoid a game if your edge is big enough. It's possible to be profitable in a high-rake game under the right circumstances. The important thing is to be *mindful* of the rake, as most players don't even factor it into their decision-making process when choosing a game.

So, now we have a grasp of all the factors that control our profitability in poker. The question is, how do we use this knowledge to actually boost profit? The key is in understanding that these six levers represent a dependent system, not six individual factors. That means improving profits isn't as simple as randomly improving in one (or multiple) areas. If you've ever felt like you were working hard on your game and doing everything right but just weren't making the progress you "deserved," chances are a deficiency in one of the areas was holding back the progress you were making in all of the other areas.

What's Your Bottleneck?

In a system of interdependent variables, a bottleneck in just one area is enough to slow down the entire system. For example, if you were the best player in the world (skill) but only played $1-$2 NL, your profits would be severely constrained. It wouldn't matter how much you improved your game (skill), how big your edge was, how often you played your A-Game (efficiency), how much you played (volume) or how low the rake was, without increasing your stakes, you wouldn't be able to make meaningful improvements to your profits.

The rake factor is also a good example of this phenomenon. A high enough rake can literally make a game unbeatable. In those circumstances, no amount of improvement in any of the other areas would make a difference. Many players get trapped in the micro stakes, because even though they have a large edge over their opponents, the high rake makes it very difficult to grind up a bankroll.

The key to using this framework to improve your profits is to take an honest look at each of the six levers and discover the lever, or combination of levers, causing your bottleneck.

Once you know what's actually holding you back, you can make the proper adjustments to remove the bottleneck and the constraint on your profits that it's causing.

CHAPTER 6

INTRODUCING A-GAME POKER

By investing in this book, and actually taking the time to read it, chances are you want something more out of the game of poker, whether that's increased profitability, moving up in stakes, a feeling of control, or quality of life improvements.

As we've discussed so far, the game has changed significantly since the early days and what it takes to be successful in today's game is much different than it used to be. I believe that in order to be successful in the modern game of poker, you must follow a system similar to the A-Game Poker System. It's what most of the top pros are doing whether they know it or not.

So, what exactly is meant by A-Game Poker? For a lot of people, it means getting in the zone, locking in, and making the best plays you can play for the entirety of your session. However, to get to the heart of the matter, we need to go a few levels deeper.

If I were to ask you why you want to play your A-Game, what would your answer be? Most players I ask have a snap reply: they want to play their A-game to make more profit. Pretty obvious, right? But this is where it gets to be a bit tricky.

What if I were to ask you why you want to optimize your profitability each time you sit down to play? That's a bit of a tougher question, one that you might have to think about for a while. I usually get a wide range of answers when I ask this. Some people talk about what they'll do with the money they make or the freedom they'll be able to buy with the money they earn.

Some talk about maximizing their earnings as a scorecard to gauge their success, scratching the competitive itch that's their reason to play. Some love the challenge of always trying to improve their game and themselves. Some cite a combination of those reasons. The point is, while everyone, at least everyone who would read a book like this, wants to optimize their profits, they all have different reasons for doing so.

So, I could have defined A-game Poker as something like maximizing your poker profits by optimizing every edge available. That would be pretty close to accurate, but it doesn't quite fit. What makes poker unique is that almost everyone who takes the game seriously does so by choice. Being a professional poker player isn't like being a doctor, lawyer, financial professional or other highly-respected professional, where you might have chosen the path because your parents pushed you to do it or it was a safe way to earn a significant income. The fact is, those who dedicate themselves to the game of poker are often bucking social norms and the expectations of their families.

Quite often, making poker their choice of profession comes with significant social resistance or downright disapproval. There are certainly easier and safer ways to earn money. Someone who has what it takes to be a big winner in poker could easily apply their skill set in other areas and do quite well for themselves. Yet there are more doctors, lawyers, and financial professionals who dream about making the switch to full-time poker pro than poker pros who dream about pursuing those professions. There's just something about the game of poker that's different. It scratches an itch that seemingly nothing else can. And, as I say, those who choose it, do so for a myriad of reasons.

Which means that "A-Game Poker" for one player does not necessarily mean the same thing as it does for another. It's what makes poker so compelling and why I wouldn't dream of prescribing a one-size-fits-all system for optimizing poker success.

What A-game Poker is really about is:

Optimizing profits in a way that achieves your personal poker vision.

And since there are hundreds of ways to maximize your poker profits, both on and off the table, some of those ways will fit into your poker vision, and some will not.

For example, if you're an online poker player, time zones can be a massive factor in your quality of life.

An MTT schedule in Europe might get started in the evening and go late into the night, while in Mexico or the west coast of North America, you might be starting early in the morning and be able to have more conventional work hours.

Moving to a place that has a more optimal schedule for your given game could be an obvious way to optimize your profits, but if you have a family and established roots, you might not want to move them halfway across the world to fit your poker schedule. So that might not be something that fits into your poker vision.

On the other hand, if you're young and just getting started, with no family and no deep roots, and your main objective is to have the highest quality of life while optimizing your profits, then moving to a different location might make perfect sense.

Deciding whether it makes more sense to play MTTs or cash games or some other form of poker again comes down to what your vision is. Cash games offer more consistency in scheduling and flexibility than MTTs, allowing for more control over when you play and who you play against. But MTTs, while requiring a bigger commitment of time and giving less scheduling flexibility, offer the promise of massive payoffs while tapping into a more competitively intense structure. So maybe that's your thing.

Another question might be, should you battle in tough games or game select? Again, this comes down to your poker vision. While in the short run, game selection might be the best way to optimize your poker profits, in the long run, battling in tough games can hone your competitive edge and increase your skill so that you can have a wider range of profits in the future.

The point is that there's a long list of ways that you can optimize your profits in poker, many of which we will discuss in this book, but what it finally comes down to is optimizing profits in a way that best achieves your personal poker vision.

Okay. You now understand the basis of A-Game Poker. But before you can figure out how to implement your personal poker vision, you need to establish exactly where you're at right now. Maybe you're going through a rough patch and you're searching for a way to stay in the game. Maybe you've had success and just want to take it to the next level. Or maybe you're doing all right in the game and want to push to become one of the highest earning players out there.

Whatever best describes you, there's a gap between where you are now and where you want to be. Because if you were just crushing it and completely comfortable in the knowledge that you're exactly where you want to be, you wouldn't be reading this book.

The goal here is to give you a framework to take you from where you are now to where you want to be. We'll help you close that performance gap and give you the tools to consistently bring your A-game to the table every time you play. The rest of this book is going to lay out a blueprint of what I see as the quote unquote "perfect" poker player. I will lay out the essential building blocks and you will choose how to incorporate them into your game to fulfill your personal vision.

The reason that poker is such an amazing game is because it offers something for everyone. You can roll into a casino after a tough week of work, sit down for a few hours at a $1-$2 game and let all your worries go while you battle for a few hours in the ring, or you can dedicate your life to being one of the best in the world. It all depends on what you want.

And while this book is primarily designed for people in the latter category, looking to be the best in the world or at least one of the best in their own little section of the game, if you're someone who only wants to be more competitive in a recreational way, there's still a lot you can get out of this book. Either way, it's time to embark on this journey and dive into The Anatomy of an A-Game Player.

PART 2

The Anatomy of an A-Game Player

As poker gets more and more competitive, you really need to be on top of all aspects of your game to compete at the highest levels. Elliot quickly identified issues I didn't even know were affecting my game and helped me deal with the most important ones. I can feel the difference every day, both when I play and in my personal life. The success I've had was in no small part because of my sessions with Elliot.

- Ben Heath - High-Stakes MTT Player with over $19,000,000 in earnings

CHAPTER 7

BUILDING AN A-GAME PLAYER

Let's try a quick visualization exercise. Take a deep breath, starting to imagine a laboratory with a table in the center.

Laying on the table is the perfect poker player—or at least what will be the perfect poker player after you are finished constructing them. You can add any attributes you like to your creation.

What skills will they possess?

What kind of demeanor and mindset?

Which mental models will they use?

Picture their daily routines, how they approach and improve their game. Consider their life off the table, how they approach each session, and what they do after playing. Close your eyes for a moment, visualize this ultimate professional poker player in full detail.

...

...

...

What do you see?

Chances are, that player was living their life in a way that maximized not only their poker profits but every aspect of their existence. They were a happy, healthy, integrated human, able to live life to the fullest. This is what I call an A-Game Player.

An A-Game Player is one who views the game in the long-term, approaches the game like an ultimate professional, has a clear vision for why they play the game, is driven to achieve that vision, has a mindset that is congruent with poker success, and consistently executes a winning strategy.

Over the years, I've had the opportunity to work with many of the game's best players. In a way, I'm in that laboratory with them, working to give them all the attributes they need to get to the top of the game and stay there long term. Because every player has a different vision of the game, none of them approach it in the exact same way. However, there are a clear set of principles, strategies, and tactics that nearly all of the best players in the world have in common, and when they decide to neglect one of these areas, they do so knowing they are leaving money on the table.

In this section I'm going to break down the Anatomy of an A-Game Player and tell you exactly what it takes to get to the top of the poker world. I understand that your vision might not include that as the goal, it isn't for everyone, but let's begin with that as the ideal, and from there you can pick and choose which aspects fit best into your personal vision of what you want. So, please, step into my lab, and let's go about answering the central question:

"What are the best in the world doing that I'm not?"

Chapter 8

Poker As a Professional Sport

There's an ongoing debate in the poker world about how the game should be described. Is it in fact a game? Or is it a sport? Perhaps it's something in between. One of the terms for poker that has gained popularity in recent years is "mind sport." But frankly, I'm indifferent. The truth is, I don't actually care how poker is defined.

What I know, and what I do care about, is that the best poker players in the world approach the game as if they are professional athletes. What exactly does it mean to approach poker as if you're a professional athlete? Well, if you think about the most successful athletes in your favorite sport, they've made success in their field their top priority. Every aspect of their life is geared toward creating and maintaining elite performance in their chosen sport.

Imagine this scenario:

Your favorite football team just signed a player to a massive contract. In the press conference announcing the signing, your stud signing talks about how hard he worked to get to where he is, but now that he's here, having made it to the top, he's just going to coast. He'll show up on game day, but he's not going to practice. In fact, when he's not actually on the field playing, he's going to be enjoying his big payday with late nights, hard partying, and a lavish lifestyle.

How do you think you'd feel about that signing? I'm guessing you wouldn't be terribly optimistic about your team's prospects for the upcoming year. However, this is the way most poker players, including the overwhelming majority of professionals, approach their careers. But it's not how the best in the world, the A-Game Players, approach the game.

The best in the world's goal is to optimize their profits and craft every aspect of their life around this goal. There are infinite ways that you can approach poker.

If you approach poker like a sport, you'll have the opportunity to be paid like a professional athlete. If you approach poker like it's a game, it'll never be more than a hobby. Which means tiny profits, breaking even, or even losing money long term.

As we discussed in the evolution of a professional poker player, you can see how this is true. In the early days of the online poker boom, the stereotypical online high stakes crusher had a reputation akin to a college frat boy: stay up all night and party, roll out of bed whenever, hop in a game, and make tons of money simply by being smarter than anyone else. However, as the game evolved and the competition got tougher, the laissez-faire party-animal approach got harder to pull off. Instead of rolling out of bed and arriving ten minutes late to a final table, the top players in the world are up hours early, taking cold plunges, hitting the gym, eating a healthy breakfast, meditating, listening to Primed Mind, watching game film of that day's opponents, looking for an edge wherever they can find it, no matter how small.

"But Elliot, what about [Insert Player Name Here], they don't do any of this stuff and look at their results!"

There certainly is a small subset of players who take everything I teach here and throw it out of the window. They smoke, they drink heavily, and ride an emotional roller coaster as they play. Some players have a depth of skill, either innate or earned with years of experience that allows them to be successful despite their flawed approach.

My rebuttal is this: How is this relevant to your situation? If you're in the one percent of the one percent of genius-level poker players, maybe you can get away with cutting corners, but if you are that type of player you would already know it, and the only reason you would be reading this book is because you understand that pairing your elite talent with A-Game Poker would allow you to reach even further heights.

Also, for players like this, their trajectory is rarely a straight up graph. The volatile genius-level player can go on some massive runs, but they likely have a few equally impressive crashes that they don't make public.

No, to get to the top and stay there, the top players, many of whom I have worked with, have realized that they need to make big shifts in the way they approach the game in order to remain at the top. There will always be exceptions, of course, but in the modern game of poker this level of professionalism and commitment will only become more and more crucial as the game evolves further.

When Fedor Holz was in the midst of his massive high roller and online poker runs in 2015, our conversations reflected his commitment to the pursuit of excellence. Whether he was searching for the best chair for long online MTT sessions or trying to find the optimal form of physical exercise (he decided on martial arts as a discipline that not only gave him improved physical stamina and confidence but honed his strategic thinking as well), he left no stone unturned.

Not everyone has the talent and drive of a Fedor Holz. And certainly, if you're starting from scratch, you don't need to put your focus on such minute details quite yet, but it does show the lengths the best in the world will go to in their pursuit of excellence.

So, if you want to start treating poker with the same level of commitment as a professional athlete, where should you get started?

I've divided the anatomy of an A-Game Player into three main categories, which I'll go over now and then discuss in more detail in the chapters to come.

First, we have off-the-table optimizations—focusing on sleep, physical fitness, nutrition, scheduling, and recovery—which create the foundation around which the A-Game Poker System is built. I like to tell my clients that the goal of the A-Game System is to optimize yourself as a human being. Playing better poker is a nice side effect.

The second category is what I call the A-Game Skill Stack—poker-specific skills like bankroll management, game selection, skill acquisition, volume, and networking.

Finally, we have in-game execution, which is the Efficiency portion that we talked about in the Six Levers of Poker Profit, namely, the percentage of time you apply the full extent of your skill during a session.

These categories are what make up the anatomy of an A-Game Player.

PRO CASE STUDY

KEVIN MARTIN

2022 STREAMER OF THE YEAR

Elliot and I started working together in 2015. I was 22 years old and maybe had a net worth of $10,000. I had no idea about hard work and discipline. I was flying by the seat of my pants, letting my natural personality and a little bit of notoriety carry my content career. Poker-wise, I was a complete failure. My work ethic was nonexistent. I had no structure.

My idea of poker pros was, 'Oh, they're probably pretty good, and they're probably getting lucky.' That's what I thought. I didn't understand the professionalism and work required to become a good poker player. I just thought some people had it, some people didn't.

Elliot didn't sugarcoat anything. I remember in one of our first sessions, he said: "Kevin, you are terrible at this game. And that's okay. The question is, what are you going to do about it?" That was a reality check. At that moment, I decided I would give it a hundred percent, and if I fell short, so be it.

The rest of the session we spent creating a blueprint for what I needed to do to have a chance to succeed. It was apparent how much work would be required and the number of sacrifices I would need to make. And I loved it!

We went through all the pillars I needed to cover. Sleep, fitness, recovery, study, and performance. I was so far behind in poker theory that we needed to take a step back and dedicate the most significant piece of the pie to that. Studying was something I knew I could do. I won Big Brother Canada because I outworked and out studied everyone in the house. I carried that over to poker and started treating the game like I was preparing for an athletic competition. And I had a blast.

With that level of focus and determination, I picked things up very quickly. Yes, it was a lot of work, but it didn't feel that way because I was having so much fun and progressing quickly. My community saw it right away. How fast I was transforming in front of their eyes. Which fueled me to keep going.

The whole experience opened my eyes to what I could do by setting a focus and putting in the repetitions every day. Since then, I wouldn't have it any other way. I realize how close I was to letting the opportunity slip through my hands. As a consequence, I now try to maintain that level of drive in the areas that are important to me. Sure, it's not as easy as it was in the beginning, and there have been plateaus along the way, but having seen the other side, I wouldn't ever go back.

And I haven't peaked yet! There are many more chapters to come. When we started, I was losing at $5 tournaments. More recently, I'd lost a $125,000 pot to Daniel Negreanu in Vegas. Sure, I wish I had won that pot, but it's pretty epic that I was in that spot. I've won Streamer of the Year, played on high-stakes shows, and I'm interacting and collaborating with some of the biggest names in the game regularly.

The losses are big, the wins are big, but I'm playing top-tier competition now. I feel confident in almost any no-limit game. I still have a lot to learn, but I'm out there battling with the big dogs. It's really cool to think about.

Especially since poker wasn't something that came naturally to me. I wasn't the guy who won big early on and used that momentum and talent to propel me into becoming a pro. I lost, and I sucked for a long time, and lots of people on the internet watched while I did it.

I won't go as far as to say anyone can achieve what I have. Still, you might be surprised just how far you can go when you become a true professional, treat the game like you're training for an athletic competition and follow along closely with what Elliot teaches. It worked for me, and I'm glad I fully bought into the program and allowed myself to make it all work.

CHAPTER 9

OFF THE TABLE OPTIMIZATION

You've probably heard the term "Work-Life Balance." It's an idea centered around the notion that the best way to achieve professional productivity is by devoting significant energy not only to your career but also to your life away from your job, i.e., hobbies, family, friends, travel, self-care, etc. The word "balance" suggests that to live a healthy life you need to offset the time you focus on your career with time focused on other areas. In effect, you are living two separate lives—work and personal—and compartmentalizing them with equal weight.

The problem with this approach is that it's not how the best in the world position themselves for success. The truth is, most of those who reach the highest level in their fields do so because they are obsessed with their craft. They are driven to succeed and will pay nearly any cost to achieve that success. Often, in pursuit of their goal, they'll neglect family, friends, health, and life experiences. This can be highly effective in the short term. Those who put in the most reps typically rise to the top. However, success achieved in this way can often be accompanied by regret, loneliness, and burnout. Reaching the top of the mountain, achievers of this type may realize that it doesn't feel as good as expected, and the "happily ever after story," they were hoping for doesn't really exist.

This is the problem "Work-Life Balance" is looking to solve. We all understand that, in addition to career accomplishments, meaningful relationships, good health and novel life experiences are essential parts of a fulfilling life. Most people view these two options in black and white. I can either sacrifice everything to become the best in the world, or I can cap my success and live a happy and balanced life. But what if there were a better way?

What if you could launch yourself along the "best in the world" trajectory, enjoy the journey, and live a fulfilled life, regardless of whether or not you reached the top of the mountain? This is the challenge I've been solving during my career as a performance coach. The single-minded approach to success works very well but has a high-casualty rate because it's hard to sustain. Even those who succeed with this method often do so with much regret. The balanced approach works well for living a happy life, but it, too, can come with regrets along the lines of "What would I have been capable of if I gave it my all?"

Here's the good news: success versus happiness is not a binary proposition. You can do both. You can reach your personal ceiling in the game, or in any area of life, and also be extremely happy and fulfilled along the way.

The better news? This outcome is actually easier to achieve and more sustainable than the all or nothing approach. An A-Game Player understands that an integration between things poker and things personal is the key to getting to the highest levels of the game and enjoying your life along the way. This goes back to the definition of A-Game Poker:

Optimizing profits in a way that achieves your personal poker vision.

The key here is optimizing your results in a way that fulfills your personal vision. I call this Performance Lifestyle Integration. If we start with the premise that everything you do in your life affects your success in poker, either positively or negatively, then *lifestyle integration* involves looking at every area of your life and figuring out how to optimize the activities that are a net positive in relation to poker.

This means you don't have to feel guilty about enjoying video games or other hobbies or spending time with your friends or family (yes, this is something real that high performers often worry about). It means that you begin to look at your life as an integrated whole and choose how to spend your time in a way that supports your goal of becoming world-class.

If you were to spend 10 hours a day six days a week on poker (an extreme example) and sleep for 8 hours per day, that still leaves you with 42 hours a week for the other areas of your life. In this chapter, we'll look at the main off-the-table areas that an A-Game Player should optimize to have the biggest impact on their on-the-table results:

- Time Management
- Sleep
- Fitness
- Nutrition
- Recovery

Time Management

Most poker players will tell you the number one reason they play the game is to have freedom. No boss. No set hours. No one telling them what to do and when to do it. That's why there's such hesitation when I ask any of my clients to implement a schedule.

Chances are you're feeling the same way right now. Maybe you even had an impulse to skip this section entirely. Freedom is an interesting word. What does it really mean? There are a few different ways to look at it. Most people think it's the ability, as I've just said, to do whatever you want, whenever you want, with no responsibilities and no one telling you what you need to be doing. My definition is a little different.

My definition of freedom is the ability to make conscious decisions about how you want to allocate your time. Most poker players come into the game thinking they want the do-whatever-you-want-whenever-you-want-to-do-it definition of freedom, but they quickly come to realize that's neither effective for achieving success in the game nor as a fulfilling way to live your life. In my view, you can either have that kind of freedom, which will limit what you can accomplish, or you can implement a schedule and accomplish *everything* you want.

But let me be clear up front: the goal of a schedule is not to create a prison. The true freedom that poker grants is really the freedom to put anything on your schedule that you want. If you're reading this book, I'm pretty sure it's because you want to accomplish something more in poker and in life. To do that, there are certain actions you *must* take—and you must take them in a purposeful way.

The goal of a schedule is to make conscious decisions about how you want to allocate your time in order to avoid subconscious impulses in the moment. If you're making your decisions on a moment-by-moment basis, your primal and subconscious impulses are going to win out more often than not. If you're deciding between putting in an hour of study or playing an hour of video games and you don't have a foundation beneath you, it's going to be much easier to choose the video games. If you're about to start a session and some friends call, asking if you want to hang out, if you haven't pre-planned how you're going to spend your time, you're more likely to go with what feels good in the moment.

Here's the thing that most people miss, though. When you're creating the schedule, *you* get to change it. A schedule doesn't lock you into a robotic life where every minute of your life is set in stone. Unlike a conventional job, poker gives you the flexibility to adjust on the fly.

Just because you have a session scheduled doesn't mean you can't go out with your friends and have a good time—as long as that's part of your poker vision. When you create a schedule, you can look back on it and see, Oh, well, I didn't hit my volume targets this month because I missed five sessions going out with friends instead of playing the scheduled session. There doesn't have to be a judgment attached one way or the other. But if you're disappointed that you didn't hit your targets, well, now you know why. You have the data.

When living a high-performance life, scheduling is a fantastic tool for consciously deciding how you spend your time. You make decisions in set planning-blocks, and it saves time and willpower throughout your week because you're not constantly having to make a decision in each moment about how you spend your time. The key phrase here is *conscious decisions*. That's what freedom is—the ability to make conscious choices about how you spend your time.

Without a schedule, it's unlikely you'll apportion your time in an optimal way, and you'll undoubtedly find yourself at the end of each month, wondering where the time went and how you got so little done. Conversely, when you consciously choose how you're going to spend your time, and set out the parameters, you'll be able to fit in everything you want and accomplish, so much so that it may surprise you.

Sleep

Sleep is one of the most important factors in optimal human performance. Physical health, cognitive performance, longevity, and emotional well-being are all intertwined with high-quality sleep. Despite the mountain of evidence to support this, many in the high-performance community still cling to the belief that sleep is for the weak, and the quickest route to success is to put in extra work while the rest of the world is sleeping.

"Grind while they sleep."

"I've got a dream more valuable than my sleep."

"I'll sleep when I'm dead."

While "hustle culture" gets a lot right when it comes to what it takes to be successful, it fails to recognize the absolute necessity of restoration and recovery. A Formula One driver can push his vehicle to the limits, but if they refuse to make a pit stop when needed, they're pretty much guaranteed to break down before the race is finished. There's a reason we evolved to sleep nearly a third of our lives, despite the vulnerability and danger that being unconscious for long periods of time poses.

Professional poker and high-quality sleep may, at first, seem like an unlikely pairing, given the highly unconventional schedule most poker players follow, with games sometimes stretching deep into the night, impossible to leave either because they're too profitable or because it's a tournament and the format won't allow it. In contrast, a conventional job allows for easier planning of quality sleep, with its consistent day-to-day routine. Since most recreational players work during the day and indulge their hobby at night, professional players often have an inverted schedule in order to sync up their working hours with the rest of the world's leisure time.

For instance, high-stakes live cash game players might participate in large private games lasting anywhere from 24 to 48 hours or more. Low to mid-stakes live cash game players typically find the best games during evenings and weekends. Online and live tournament players face unique challenges with no set end-time for their day, and often with a tight window between finishing one day late at night and starting early on the next.

The key with sleep is to look at it both as a long-term optimization and as a short-term edge. Long-term, quality sleep is the foundation of good health and optimal mental performance. As a short-term edge, think back to the efficiency lever that we discussed in the Six Levers of Poker Profits. If you find yourself 48 hours into a session of an amazing game that you had prepared for by getting quality sleep during the week leading up to it (because you *knew* it had the potential to go that deep), you're going to be in a much better spot than anyone who didn't plan ahead.

If you're playing a full schedule at the World Series of Poker and you emphasize sleep and recovery, while the competition indulges in the Vegas nightlife, you're going to be in a much better spot, as the series progresses, to play to your full potential while everyone else is turning into a poker zombie.

In a game in which mental acuity and decision making are key, sleep is the fuel that gives you the energy to run that engine. If you choose the life of a professional poker player, there's a good chance that, at least part of the time, you will not be able to have a conventional and fully optimized sleep schedule. The key here is to put yourself in a better position than your opposition, stacking as many edges as possible in your favor. Quality sleep ranks high on the list of areas where you can find an advantage.

Nutrition

Nutrition is one of the most highly debated topics in the high-performance world. I have no doubt that what we eat affects how we perform, as I've had clients both improve and destroy their performance by making changes in their nutrition plans. There are many who deny this connection, arguing that while diet and nutrition are critical to physical performance, they have little to no effect in a mental competition such as poker. No reasonable person would argue that a fast-food meal washed down with a large soda is going to be better for you and for your optimal performance than a whole-food nutrient-rich meal prepared simply and without deep-frying.

Imagine two players with equal skill levels playing a full schedule at the World Series of Poker. The first fuels themself exclusively with fast food, sugar-filled energy drinks and sodas. The second has high-quality, whole foods, prepared for them and delivered at optimal intervals. Which one of these players would you rather buy action from?

We've all had the experience of having the food we eat affect how we feel and think. Think of that hefty lunch causing a late afternoon crash. Food companies pay teams of scientists large sums of money to design foods that make customers feel a certain way, and it would be foolish to assume that the fuel we put in our body has no impact on our ability to perform at poker, both in the short and long term.

An A-Game Player's nutrition plan optimizes for long-term health, short-term performance, and it does so in a way that minimizes the amount of time you'll need to be thinking about this area of your life. Of course, if you spend too little time on it, you'll end up making poor decisions, either by not fueling yourself or by choosing easy options that are quick and thoughtless. But put too much of a focus on it and you'll wind up spending time and energy on nutrition that could be better spent improving your game by actually playing or recovering.

Fitness

While my experience of working with the best players makes me confident that nutrition has a significant impact on poker performance, I am even more certain about the importance of physical fitness. If you take a look around the typical poker table, there's little chance you'll confuse your opponents for highly-trained, physically fit athletes. For most of the game's history, "physical fitness" and "poker" have been as unlikely to appear in the same sentence as "the Sahara Desert" and "snow."

The nature of the poker lifestyle has historically made it the antithesis of good physical fitness, especially among those who play the game for a living. Sitting in front of a computer all day or in an unergonomic casino chair, wolfing down unhealthy snacks, means that poker players have a lot of catching up to do if they want to maintain even a base level of physical fitness. In the past, you wouldn't ever have expected to see a table full of physical specimens gathered around a poker table unless it was on the airplane of an NBA team traveling between cities. However, over the past few years there has been a dramatic shift. The players who consistently make the final tables on the Super High Roller tournament scene are buff and ripped. This is no coincidence.

High-stakes players must find every edge available and optimize it to the best of their abilities. When nobody at the table was physically fit, you could get away with being out of shape, but once a few of the best players started exploiting this edge, the rest needed to follow suit. If you wander by the hotel gym before a major final table, you'll see most of the participants sweating it out, preparing their minds and bodies for the challenges ahead.

Embracing exercise is not just about physical health; it's one of the most potent performance enhancers in a player's arsenal. If you want to be an A-Game Player, optimizing physical fitness is an absolute priority. Obviously, you don't need to have the physique of a bodybuilder or the 40-time of an NFL athlete or have the VO2 max of a Tour de France competitor. But if you want to compete at the highest levels, it's essential to start a workout routine that optimizes your fitness.

Beyond the performance benefits you'll derive from improved fitness, you'll reduce your risk of all major chronic diseases, increase your day-to-day quality of life, and add to your expected lifespan. Poker, by its nature, is sedentary, requiring long hours of physical inactivity. To be blunt, it's not a healthy pursuit in terms of physical wellbeing. Even if you're in good shape now, without a proper fitness system in place, your body will decline, month after month, year after year, and with that physical decline will come decreases in cognitive function, stamina, energy, mental resilience and focus.

An A-Game Player understands the edge that can be gained from high levels of physical fitness, which will decrease stress and anxiety while increasing both *efficiency* and the amount of quality *volume* you're able to sustain—two of the most critical levers of poker profits.

Recovery

I define recovery as any activity that restores your physical, mental, or emotional energy levels. For those who have fully embraced the "A-Game" lifestyle, this is often the most difficult area to implement, and I often find myself stressing again the importance of this area to my clients. This is particularly true for younger players and those who are still in the honeymoon phase of their poker journey. Poker has a unique ability to seep into your mind at all hours of the day, and many of the best in the world go through periods where they have poker on their mind 24/7. There are certainly seasons in your poker career where this is perfectly healthy and even optimal for making large progressions in skill acquisition.

Poker takes a significant amount of physical, mental, and emotional energy to be able to compete at the highest level. During these seasons of obsession, it's possible to compensate for the energy you're expending even if you're neglecting some of the recommended recovery steps. However, these seasons of obsession don't last forever, and it's easy to make the mistake of thinking you can push through without focusing on recovery time. That's when disaster can strike and burnout can occur.

The best example of this phenomenon is what happens during the six weeks of the World Series of Poker. Playing a full schedule in Vegas is the ultimate endurance test for poker players. Between bracelet events, off-site tournaments, and cash games, you can literally play poker round-the-clock. The action is truly amazing. Not to mention the Vegas nightlife in which so many players indulge, also conveniently available 24/7. What it means is that for a six-week marathon of long days and longer nights, you have an opportunity to jump into action as soon as you bust out of your main tournament for the day and keep going and going and going.

The excitement and pageantry of the series can fuel many players for the first two weeks. But after that, if you pay close attention, you'll discover a mob of poker zombies stumbling around from tournament to cash game and back again, players who are no longer playing their A-game and in fact might be all the way down to C-level. These players think the games are so good that they still have a large edge, but the truth is, in the state they're in, they probably rate to lose, and at best maybe break even. So, while it's tempting to push a full schedule seven days a week at an event like the WSOP, the only way to maintain the high edges that are possible for the full slate, is if you schedule time for recovery.

It reminds me a bit of my work with MMA fighters. The type of fighter that chooses to work with me is usually extremely driven, often to their own detriment. They're so obsessed with improving that they push their bodies, often putting in two or three training sessions per day at the gym, seven days per week.

While putting in the reps is how you get to be the best in the world, there comes a point of diminishing returns. When you continue to push past that point not only do you risk regression, you're also wasting time that could be better spent elsewhere. For this type of driven fighter, true discipline involves taking a break from training.

This is an easier concept to accept for athletes engaged in a physical sport. For mental athletes, the warning signs are more subtle, at least until the point where you fully melt down and spew off a large chunk of your bankroll. If you're reading this book, it's likely because you're driven to become the best you can possibly be. That drive is rare and one of the most valuable assets you have. To be an A-Game Player, it's necessary to understand that there comes a point, though, where your drive can do more harm than good, and you need to set aside time for recovery.

CHAPTER 10

A-GAME SKILL STACK

When you look at the most successful and highest-paid individuals in any industry, those at the top typically get there by being more proficient than almost anyone else in the world in the key area that defines the industry. In the case of poker, that area is absolute poker skill. Additionally, the ones that separate themselves from the pack have additional skills that complement the main skill, making them exponentially more valuable.

CEOs are hired to be brilliant business strategists, but the best of the best are inspirational leaders and have an uncanny ability to sell their vision to investors and the public. A software engineer can get paid very well for being an elite coder, but their earning potential skyrockets when they pair that skill with a deep understanding of what the customer wants and the ability to communicate clearly with nontechnical managers and executives. The best baker in the world may sell a lot of cakes locally, but when they pair that mastery of their craft with an ability to market themselves, they can go from a local legend to global icon.

Let's take a look at some examples from the sports world:

At his peak Conor McGregor was certainly one of the best and most exciting fighters in the world. He also had a set of skills—mainly charisma, showmanship, and fighting style—that catapulted him into the ranks of highest-earning athletes in the world, in a sport where most fighters would be lucky to even crack the top 100. There's no doubt he was a talented fighter, but it was the other skills and attributes he possessed that allowed him to enter the elite levels of earnings.

At the time of the writing of this book, the baseball player Shohei Ohtani is poised to sign one of the biggest contracts in professional sports history. With an expected contract value over six hundred million, it would be the second- largest contract in sports history, extra impressive given that MLB ranks only fourth in average pay per player. Ohtani is unique in that he is both one of the five best hitters in the game, as well as one of the five best pitchers in the game. For those not familiar with baseball, pitchers do not hit. Pitching and hitting are considered completely different skill sets, and at the time of writing this Ohtani is the only MLB player who gets regular playing time at both.

In addition to this, Ohtani is incredibly likable and charismatic, which, when combined with his elite skills, make him the most marketable player in the game. The amount of merchandise and tickets that he sells alone, allows the teams that sign him to happily pay that massive price tag, driving his value through the roof.

In any industry, it is rare that being the best at a single skill will earn you the most money. This same principle holds true in poker.

If you've been in the game long enough, you likely know a player who is extremely talented yet often broke. In fact, there is an entire industry built around keeping these types of players in action. Owners of poker backing groups are often some of the wealthiest participants in the poker industry, even if they never actually play a hand. This isn't only because they have access to capital, they also help these skilled players by filling the holes in their skill set, through coaching, forced game selection and bankroll management, dictated by the terms of their staking agreement.

In poker, much of your success will be dictated by your approach off the table. In the previous section we covered the more general, non poker specific areas that have a significant impact on your game. Here, we'll dive into the most important poker-specific skills you can cultivate as an A-Game Player. This list certainly is not exhaustive. As with elite athletes, entrepreneurs and executives, the skill stack necessary to reach the top is extensive and nuanced. The ones I cover here are what I have discovered to be the common denominator among the best players in the world.

Bankroll Management

One of the least sexy topics in all of poker, bankroll management, which also makes it one of the most important ones.Bankrolls are the lifeblood of any business, and your bankroll is the lifeblood of your poker career. Many good businesses fail because of poor financial management, and many excellent poker players go broke for the same reason.

Legendary investor Warren Buffet has two rules for investing:

"The first rule of an investment is don't lose [money]. And the second rule of an investment is don't forget the first rule. And that's all the rules there are."

As much as we would like to try, we can't quite follow those rules in poker, but I would amend them to something like this:

The first rule of bankroll management is always stay in action. And the second rule of bankroll management is don't forget the first rule.

One of the most critical of the Six Levers of Poker Profits is stakes. The stakes you can play profitably dictate how much you are able to earn from the game. If the best player in the world were somehow forced to play no higher than 2-5 NL for the rest of their life, they would make significantly less money than the tenth worst player in the world playing 1000/2000 NL against the nine players in the world who were even worse than him.

It is as possible to be too conservative with your bankroll as it is to be too aggressive. Your bankroll is an asset you use to earn profits, and an A-Game Player knows how to properly deploy that asset to optimize their returns.

Game Selection

Mediocre players have become wealthy through disciplined game selection. Elite players have gone broke through reckless game selection. If we had the ability to look at the top 100 earners in poker from the past year while simultaneously quantifying the top 100 most skilled players, I'd wager you'd be surprised at how different the two lists were.

Typically professional competitions are all about the best facing off against the best, with the winner taking home the prize pool, or earning a contract based on performance. Game selection is like Lebron James getting paid by points scored and having the ability to choose the level of competition he wants to play against. Sure, he'd probably do quite well in a game versus an All-Star team, but if he chose to play against a team of high school freshmen, he would absolutely demolish them.

In athletics you need to beat the best in the world to earn the highest possible income. In poker you just need to beat the players sitting across from you, and those can be other elite players or players who barely know the rules of the game. Edge just might be the Lever of Poker Profit that has the most leverage behind it.

Now, obviously it's not as simple as always being able to find a game vs barely functioning players. Game selection is a skill, and an A-Game Player understands that the chances at a long and prosperous career are greatly increased by cultivating it.

Networking

Poker is an individual competition that is optimized by working with a team. The ability to connect with other players in the poker community is one of the most valuable skills you can add to your stack. Working with a group of like-minded individuals allows you to improve at a rate much greater than any individual could on their own.

Think of this like an MMA Fighter. During competition a fight is just about as individual as it gets. However, in the lead up to the fight there is an entire team that works together to prepare the fighter for combat. Yes, there are coaches for fight technique, nutrition, strength training, even mindset. There are also other fighters brought in to serve as training partners, fighters you might even have to face in the cage somewhere down the line. However, in the gym steel sharpens steel and the group comes together to make everyone better.

There's a very similar dynamic in poker. Nearly all of the most successful players I've worked with have a core group of friends they work together with to rapidly improve one another's games. They do this despite the possibility of occasionally being confronted at the table by someone who will have deep insight into their thought processes, willing to make this trade-off because of the upside that comes from sharing their knowledge with one another.

Skill Acquisition

We've discussed how the technical side of poker keeps evolving at a rapid pace. There was a point where you could be profitable based solely on your innate intelligence and good instincts. But in today's game, those qualities will only get you so far. The best players in modern poker are those who acquire and improve skill at the fastest pace. It's not just those who put in the most work that come out on top; it's those who are most efficient and effective with the time they spend on study.

We're still at the point where many players think watching a training video or a Twitch stream counts as study. The reality is, if you're not actively engaged in the training, what you're doing is just entertainment. The *process* you use to improve your skills is just as important as the skills themselves. An A-Game Player understands that a deep, focused, study session working on spots that happen regularly is drastically more valuable than randomly reviewing hands or watching videos focusing on spots that only occur a few times a year.

CHAPTER 11

IN-GAME EXECUTION

A common mistake that most poker players make when calculating earnings and forecasting their profits is assuming a best-case scenario. At the end of the year when they fall short of their expectations, they'll blame it on luck, and then make the exact same mistake the following year. What they've failed to factor in is that they won't always be playing their best, and so they greatly overestimate their edge when playing less than their A-Game. Just as you have a strategy for playing your cards, if you want to maximize your Efficiency Lever, then you need a strategy for applying your strategy.

I've identified three key mindsets that A-Game Players use as the foundation for in-game execution. A "mindset" here is defined as a filter we put on external information that informs our internal decision-making. There are an infinite number of ways we can filter the events at a poker table, and how we choose to filter those events has a massive impact on our execution.

You Are the Casino

Everyone knows that poker is a long-term game. Yet very few actually understand variance and how that affects the range of outcomes that are possible over any given amount of time. The most frustrating and simultaneously beautiful part of poker is that the external result can vary massively from the expected outcome of a decision.

In nearly every other competition, both physical and mental, we get close to real time feedback on the quality of our actions. Shoot a free throw in basketball—did it go in or not? If yes, you did it right, if no, then you have an adjustment to make. Playing chess, did your opponent capture a key piece in a way you didn't expect? Then you made a miscalculation along the way. Make a pass in football that misses its intended target? Well, you didn't put the ball where it needed to be. So, while there can be a nominal amount of variance in these activities, it's small enough that it flattens very quickly.

Poker is a different animal entirely. To be successful you must have the ability to craft a strategy that is theoretically profitable. You must also have the fortitude to apply that theory over a long enough period of time to test its viability. In that sense, you're more like the house taking bets in a casino.

Imagine this:

You're a big player looking to have a fun night of blackjack after closing a massive business deal. You're playing $500 a hand and you start out hot. Blackjack after blackjack, the chips start piling up on your side. You're up $25,000 when you notice something strange.

All of a sudden, the pit boss tells the dealer to start hitting on 18 when you have a 9 or 10 showing and stand when the dealer has a 15 or 16—both plays that are negative EV for the house. You're not sure what's going on, but you're excited, as your $25,000 quickly grows to $50,000. Next, the pit boss instructs the dealer to start paying you out 2:1 on your blackjacks, a more favorable rate than the typical 3:2 that is standard. You're not sure what's going on, but you keep playing until you're eventually up a boatload, at which point you call it a night so you can hit the town with your winnings.

Does it sound ridiculous and unrealistic that a casino would change the rules of a game in favor of the players to try to win back money from them? Of course, it does.

Yet, it's exactly what you, as a player, do when you change to a worse strategy based on winning or losing during a session. For recreational players, poker is a leisure activity similar to blackjack, sports betting, or going to the movies. A-Game Players have the unique opportunity to play the role of the house. And this is exactly where the "You Are the Casino" mindset comes into play.

The casino gets to set the rules of the game such that they have a minimum edge no matter what happens. With that edge in place, they don't care what happens in a single hand of blackjack, or slot machine pull. In fact, they love it when a player wins big. Walk into any casino and you'll see advertisements plastered everywhere showing all the biggest winners. That's because they know they are printing money with every spin of the roulette wheel, hand of blackjack, or pull on a slot machine. They might lose money on a particularly bad day, but they never consider changing to a sub-optimal strategy because of it. If you play big enough, they'll even fly you out, put you up in a nice suite, comp all of your meals, and get you table service at the most exclusive club. The only time they won't welcome you in is if they feel you've figured out a way to get an advantage against them or are willing to wager enough that the variance could impact their ability to host games in the future.

This is how an A-Game Player views poker. They've crafted a strategy to give them an edge on the competition, and they won't waver from it for anything but strategic reasons. They understand that the opportunity for their opponents to win in the short term allows them to make a career from the game in the long run. They view winning and losing in terms of months, years, and decades rather than in terms of hands and sessions.

Every Hand Is a New Puzzle

The "You Are the Casino" mindset is designed to put the focus on the long-term nature of the game. Yet an A-Game Player also realizes the importance of executing each hand to the best of their ability. If you assume you have a given edge, yet don't focus on consistent execution, then chances are you'll be closer to a recreational player than you will be to the house.

While you can't control the results in any given hand, you can control your execution. The "Every Hand is a New Puzzle" mindset helps keep your focus on the hand you're playing.

When you're in a session, an A-Game Player makes it their goal to play each hand to the full extent of their skill, regardless of the situation. Each hand presents you with questions that demand answers. You have a set of variables in front of you...

- Stack sizes
- Opponents' Positions
- Your range
- Your opponents' range
- Your opponents' tendencies

Whatever happened in the previous hand is irrelevant, other than as data points for understanding your opponents' ranges and tendencies. Maybe last hand you were chip leader in a massive MTT, then lost a massive pot and are now down to "just" 10BB. This is where you have an option. You can punt the 10BB stack because it feels so insignificant compared to when you had the chip lead, then complain afterward about how unlucky you got and how you deserved to win the tournament. Or you can approach the next hand as a new puzzle you must solve with the limitation of your 10BB stack.

This also holds true when you're playing for significantly less money or significantly more money than you're used to. If you're playing these games for a good reason, and your goal is to win as much money as possible, then your job is to focus on solving the puzzle in front of you regardless of what the external situation may be. Most poker players will experience a time when they're playing for much lower stakes then they're used to. Maybe this is due to bankroll considerations or because they're the only games available to fill the volume you're trying to reach. Many poker players struggle in this situation because the level of arousal is so much lower, making it harder to focus.

This is where an A-Game Player switches from simply trying to beat the game, to trying to beat the game for as much as humanly possible. They do this by applying the "Every Hand is a New Puzzle" mindset, with the variable of trying to maximize their win rate as the goal.

Playing stakes much higher than you're used to can also cause issues. If you've made a sound decision to take a shot at a big game, then it's essential to apply this mindset and not worry about the implications outside of the game. If the amount of money that's on the line is a variable that starts to factor into your decision making, that's a clear sign you're in a game you shouldn't be. Like every other decision that you make within a poker session, whether or not the game itself suits you is one more decision that you should make dispassionately and with the best long-term optimal play outcome in mind.

Poker is a long-term game in which winning is determined by consistently making the best and most correct decisions (even the small ones), regardless of short-term outcomes.

PRO CASE STUDY

BERRI SWEET

#1 HEADS-UP PLAYER IN THE WORLD

My general approach to poker most of my career has been to play every waking minute of every day. Things like working on my game, trying to get reasonable sleep, or working out and eating well to improve my performance haven't been secondary considerations— they've been nonexistent. Why would I not play poker when I have the option to play poker?

I knew I had many issues with my mental game, and I knew Elliot had good credentials. But I didn't know exactly what he was doing. I didn't know exactly how he would be able to help me. And I was doing "good enough." (All of these reasons are obviously very stupid and not actual reasons not to reach out.) So, I postponed contacting him, over and over.

Eventually, I had a stretch of lousy sleep combined with bad results and ended up burning out (for the second time in a short time). At this point, I felt physically worse than ever before, which seemed like an excellent reason to discover what would happen if I started working with a mental game coach.

Elliot and I focused on improving in two areas. The first was my professionalism towards the game. I was paying a heavy physical toll with how I approached the game. Poor sleep, low physical activity, and no outlets for releasing stress meant that my results in poker were costing me considerably from a physical standpoint. While I could do very well with that approach for a time, it just wasn't sustainable from a poker and life perspective.

Second was focusing on taking full advantage of my edge, finding more spots where I could bring my A-Game. I view long, high-stakes heads-up matches as MMA fights between brains. I've always been motivated by the competitive aspect of poker rather than the monetary side, which has served me well at times. But there are spots where it causes me to play well below expectation. It's tough for me to play my best when I have good results against someone whom I expect to have almost no chance against me.

During those sessions, I'll take my foot off the pedal, zone out, and lose focus. Playing 6-max, you don't often keep track of who you're winning or losing against. All that matters is the bottom line. But in heads-up, there is only one player you can make money from. And oftentimes, it is someone you are talking to between sessions, setting up a schedule with and getting to know.

Whenever I would have a long winning streak in a heads-up match, I would feel increasingly unhappy. Sometimes, I would feel like I was running unfairly hot. Sometimes, I would feel like it was too easy and start feeling bad for the person I was playing. I love the game when both players are landing punches, and there is an interesting metagame and lots of chaos. But winning every flip or getting every cooler felt like punching a guy lying on the floor.

Essentially, I was putting an artificial cap on my win rate based on an emotional response to what I felt was "fair." Obviously, this leads to worse play, and because poker is poker, I would start losing money back. Once I started losing, my mindset always shifted back to fight mode, but I burned too much EV before that happened.

Because of my competitive nature, I've always known I play my best when losing. After working with Elliot, I'm now able to tap into that energy at a much higher frequency, even when I'm up and would typically be more complacent. By consistently providing me with rational reasons as to why my thinking got flawed and reinforcing my otherwise very present fighting spirit, Elliot helped me get to a point where results started having minimal bearing on the quality of my play. Instead of it just being a competition against my opponent, I'm competing against past versions of myself. The game is more about seeing how high I can get my win rate and less about the opponent in front of me.

And in the 18 months since I started talking to Elliot, I have yet to have what I would classify as a downswing. Working with him also came with the added benefit of starting to run really hot. Keep doing things that make you run hot—life advice.

Focus Is a Choice

Poker is a game of incomplete information. Those who can collect the most information possible have a significant advantage over the competition.

We've seen situations where cheating is involved in a game and players were able to see their opponent's hole cards. With this level of information, even an extremely poor player can dominate the best players in the world. There's no amount of poker skill that would allow you to compensate for this amount of information disadvantage.

Now imagine the opposite. Let's say you played in a game where you didn't get to see your hole cards or the cards on the board. Chances are, even if you were the best player in the world, you wouldn't be profitable against a table of randoms if they weren't similarly handicapped.

While we would never condone any level of cheating or unethical play, your goal should be to collect as much information as possible while at the tables.

Focus is how you turn attention into information. When you're playing, you have the choice to decide how focused you want to be in any given situation. The more focus you choose to apply, the more information you'll be able to collect, and the more informed your decision will be.

An A-Game Player has the mindset of "Focus is a Choice" and chooses to deploy it as optimally as possible. Now, that might not mean you choose to deploy 100 percent locked-in focus every minute you're sitting at the table. There are limits to our ability to stay focused for long periods of time, and spending that in low-value spots may hurt your ability to deploy it in high-value situations.

Many of the strategies we discussed in the Off-The-Table Optimizations section are about increasing your capacity to focus, making it as large as possible. What applying the "Focus is a Choice" mindset means is that an A-Game Player understands that focus is not something that just magically happens, it is a choice to cultivate the skill and to apply it when necessary.

"Getting in the Zone" doesn't have to be something that happens by serendipity, it's not a magical or rare state you just stumble upon, it's a skill that starts with a choice. When you play, you can choose to observe, collect and make sense of the most important information revealed by your opponents, or you can choose to place your focus elsewhere in the hand.

The choice you make will determine how much of your skill you're able to apply, and how much in profits you'll be able to earn.

CHAPTER 12

FROM KNOWLEDGE TO ACTION

At the start of this book I said I wrote this book for those who are willing to do what it takes to be successful in poker. As we conclude The Anatomy of An A-Game Player, you should now have a clear understanding of what that looks like.

For some of you, this is where you get off the train. Some of you picked up this book because you were curious to know what the best in the world do differently, what sets them apart from the competition. If that is you, you now know the answer, and I hope you've enjoyed peeking inside the mind of the game's best.

Wait, still here? I'm guessing that means you're not just here to learn about what the best in the world do, you're here to take that knowledge, implement it in your game, and secure your position as an A-Game Player. In that case, roll up your sleeves. Because this is where the fun begins. It's where you go from hoping that you get better results, to starting to fill the gap between you and the best in the world. It's where we go from learning to doing. From watching on the sidelines to getting on the field and playing.

In the next section, I'll be sharing many of my best systems, strategies and tactics for becoming an A-Game Player. At the end of each section you'll find an "A-Game Exercise," so that the next time you sit down to play you can start implementing what you've learned.

The time to be a spectator is over. I won't make you any promises on what will happen when you implement these strategies in your game, but I can promise you that nothing will change if you take no action. You're welcome to read this book for entertainment, but make no mistake, if all you do is read, that's all you'll get from this.

Your first step in your journey to being an A-Game player is to get a notebook ready or create a digital document dedicated to completing the exercises you'll find in the next section. I suggest you fully complete each exercise before moving on to the next chapter, so you'll get the most out of this. A-Game Players take action. I'm excited by the possibilities in store for you when you begin installing these systems in your game.

Onward to "Becoming an A-Game Player."

PART 3

BECOMING AN A-GAME PLAYER

Making the WSOP Main Event Final Table is every poker player's dream, and it's hard to understand the pressure and intensity of the moment until you experience it yourself. Working with Elliot on the final table allowed me to stay calm, maintain focus, and execute the plays that led me to win it all for $8,150,000.

-Scott Blumstein - 2017 WSOP Main Event Champion

Chapter 13

The A-Game Engine

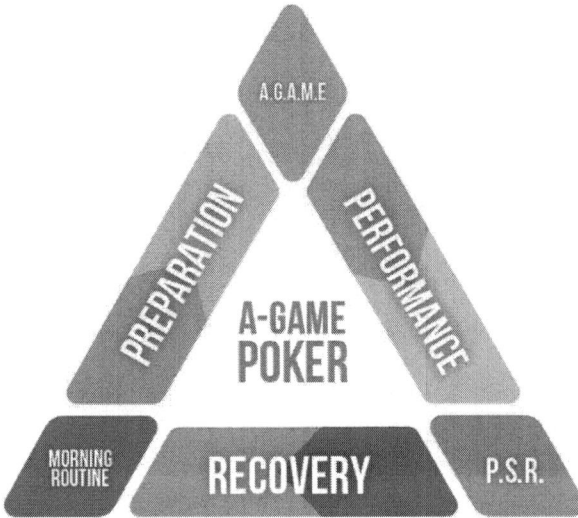

So far, we've discovered the definition of A-Game Poker and dissected the Anatomy of an A-Game Player. You know what the best players in the world are doing to reach the highest levels of the game. Now it's time to discover some highly actionable strategies and frameworks you can begin to implement today to start your journey to becoming an A-Game Player.

The A-Game Engine is my framework for taking the Fundamental Performance Question--"What Are the Best Players in the World Doing that I'm Not"—and turning it into a step-by-step system you can implement in your daily regimen as a poker player.

Included above is a graphic of the A-Game Engine, simplified for the book. (The A-Game Poker Masterclass goes deeper into the nuances of the Engine, so if you find that implementing the pieces in the book adds value to your game, then diving in deeper via the Masterclass is the logical next step.)

Notice that the A-Game Engine is divided into three phases:

1. Preparation
2. Performance
3. Recovery

And that in between each of the phases is a transition:

The A-GAME Pre-Session Protocol

The PSR, or Post-Session Routine

The Morning Routine

The key to the system is that an A-Game Player is always in one of the three phases. Making a conscious decision about the phase they are in, and choosing the optimal action for the situation, allows them to make deliberate progress in the direction of their vision. The purpose of the transitions is to facilitate a smooth transfer from one phase to the next. A player caught between phases splits their focus, preventing them from doing either phase well. For example, you can't fully recover if you're still in performance mode, which is why we use the PSR to cool down after a stretch in Performance.

To get a further understanding of the model, let's walk through each step.

1. Preparation

The preparation phase is all about building a foundation that maximizes your opportunities when it's time for Performance. The greatest separation between an A-Game Player and everyone else is how they approach the Preparation phase. Examples of this are managing your energy, improving your technical skills, optimizing your edge with soft skills such as bankroll management, networking and game selection.

"Every battle is won or lost before it is ever fought." Sun Tzu - *The Art of War*

In between Preparation and Performance is the A-Game Pre-Session Protocol. This is a warm-up routine that directs all your focus from Preparing into Performing optimally.

2. Performance

Once we are in Performance it's all about maintaining quality execution for the duration of the phase. Ideally, we perform to our fullest abilities the entire time, or at least maintain an acceptable edge even if our quality of play diminishes. After Performance is over, we use the Post-Session Routine to disconnect and shift our focus away from Performance and into Recovery.

3. Recovery

Optimal performance has a high demand of energy. To replenish energy and be an A-Game Player over the long-term, you must properly recover. We do this through restorative sleep, breaks, anti-focus time, and other activities such as meditation and visualization. Coming full circle, we use a Morning Routine, or other preparation routines to go from Recovery into Preparation.

Putting it All Together

Merriam-Webster defines a system as:

A regularly interacting or interdependent group of items forming a unified whole.

For an A-Game Player, that unified whole means utilizing the game of poker to achieve your life's vision. With the A-Game Engine, the most important principle to take away is that for the system to function properly you must always be in Preparation, Performance, or Recovery.

This requires consciously selecting the activities you are taking in a way that feeds the entire system. There are no magical routines or habits that you have to execute in order to be a successful poker player. The point is to find activities that serve the ultimate purpose of optimizing your success in poker, while being integrated into your life's vision.

Take video games as an example. I can think of many situations where playing video games can directly conflict with your goal of becoming an A-Game Player. I can also think of many situations where video games can be a healthy and beneficial way to recover the energy you spent during an intense poker session.

The difference between an A-Game Player and everyone else is that the A-Game Player is intentional in the actions they choose to fuel their A-Game Engine. The engine gives you a framework to help decide if your actions are a positive or negative when it comes to achieving your vision.

You can ask yourself the following questions:

Does this action fall into the Preparation, Performance, or Recovery Phase?

Is there a subconscious program that might be tricking me into believing it does?

(You'll learn more about these Detrimental Mental Programs later)

If you have a clear answer for question one, and can answer No to question two, then you have an activity that is potentially a good addition to your A-Game Engine. From there, we can go on to ask an additional question to not only ensure we have "good" additions to our Engine, but to have the optimal additions.

Is there something else I could be doing in its place that achieves the same goal in a more optimal way?

Let's use a preparation activity as an example. In working on improving your poker game you could have watching poker training videos as your activity. When examining this activity, ask yourself the question I posed above. In answer, the first change you might make is to watch those same videos while taking notes. Both are preparation activities, but the latter is far more optimal than the former. In this particular case, you've upgraded the activity and will be able to see benefits across the entire A-Game system.

Following from there, you ask the same question about the new activity and come up with the alternative option of spending that time with a study group discussing high-leverage spots informed by solver outputs. If you decide this is a more optimal use of your time, then another upgrade has been made. As you repeat this process across all areas of the engine, each slot must fight for its worthiness and your system evolves into a highly effective tool for achieving your poker goals and living your life's vision.

This section of the book is all about giving you a starting point where you can begin this process of iterating your A-Game system, so you're not starting out from scratch. I've included the foundational components of the system. Ones that you can begin to implement immediately and notice the impact on your game. We've discussed many times how the goal of A-Game Poker is to use poker as a tool to live your life's vision, so that's where we'll get started with building your A-Game Engine.

CHAPTER 14

THE POWER OF VISION

Think back to when you started reading this book, back to the definition we came up with for A-Game Poker.

Optimizing profits in a way that achieves your personal poker vision.

The optimizing profits side is easy for most people to grasp. Chances are that's why you're reading this book right now. Vision, by its nature, is a bit more abstract. It's a word that gets thrown around a lot in the personal development world, yet very few people truly understand what it is or its power to improve performance. And therein lies the power of vision.

In the business world, a visionary is someone able to see a world in their mind and take actions that transform that vision into reality. Visionaries are revered because it's such a difficult task—taking something that most people didn't think was possible and turning it into reality.

The biggest mistake people make is that they confuse vision with goals. You ask someone what their life's vision is and they say something like:

"I want a lot of money, a big house, fancy toys, and the ability to travel and create a happy family."

Or they might get even more specific with something like:

"I want five million in the bank and a house by the beach."

The problem with these statements is that they talk about end states rather than states of being. A goal is an end state:

"I want to win twenty-five buy-ins this month."

"I want to make three hundred thousand from poker this year."

"I want to lose thirty pounds."

"I want to bench press two hundred and twenty-five pounds."

"I want to win the WSOP Main Event."

A vision is a state of being.

"User-friendly personal computers in everyone's pocket." (Apple iPhones)

"Safe and sustainable transportation through electric vehicles and automated driving." (Tesla Motors)

"The ability to choose what I focus my attention on without worrying about the constraints of time and money."

"A strong, supportive family and social circle that is driven by improving each other's lives."

"Maintaining a sense of excitement and curiosity in poker through personal development and by solving ever more difficult puzzles."

The job of a goal is to inform the actions you take and to give you a concrete target to see if those actions are effective. The job of a vision is to inform the direction your actions take you. Goals are waypoints in your journey to living your vision, but without a vision they are aimless.

Have you ever accomplished something you've been working hard at for a very long time? It probably felt fantastic at first, but after the excitement wore off, you probably returned to your baseline and maybe even felt worse now that you no longer had something big on the horizon. This is the principle I call…

Happily Ever After Doesn't Exist

That might sound grim on the surface, but all it means is that there is no one big accomplishment that, once you achieve it, will allow you to feel permanently fulfilled. That's a trap that nearly all poker players fall into at some point or another.

"I'll be happy when I get my first six-figure tournament win."

"I'll be happy once I'm playing high stakes."

"I'll be happy once I buy this house."

"I'll be happy when I get my first seven-figure tournament win."

"I'll be happy when my bankroll reaches $100,000."

Goal-focused happiness indicators never produce long-term results, and I don't use the word "never" lightly here. In my decade plus of working with the best in the world, both in poker and other high-performance industries, I have not once had a client achieve a goal and live happier ever after. I strongly doubt I ever will.

That's because without a strong vision, achievements have no meaning. If we have no state of being we are working towards, then we have no compass, no way of knowing if we are going in the right direction. This is especially true in a game like poker, where the value you add to the world comes from the person you became through your efforts in the game. It can be very difficult to separate the idea of a vision from the ideas of a goal. This is why I define vision as:

Your mental model of the best version of yourself.

Achieving our full potential is how we gain our greatest personal fulfillment, while making our biggest contribution to the world. Your vision is your best attempt to solidify what that best version of yourself looks like, so you can consistently strive to reach that potential.

You will never know exactly what that best version of yourself looks like, however, because there are so many variables, paths, and outcomes. Trying to follow one static road will only limit you. That's why your vision is not a static destination. It is instead your best attempt to understand who you are and where your unique talents, abilities, and motivations lie.

Creating a vision is a process that requires a lot of introspection, reflection, and refinement. It's so important that I devote an entire module in my A-Game Poker Masterclass going through what I call the Vision Mapping Process.

We'll begin here with a simple exercise to help you create your first vision statement. Nearly all major companies have a vision statement, the main goal which is to get everyone in the company aligned on the same mission, and to let the world know what it is that the company is striving to create through its products and services. Your personal poker vision statement is similarly all about charting a map of the world you aim to create for yourself through the game of poker.

A-Game Exercise: Crafting Your Vision Statement

Exercise time. Pull out your notebook or document, set a timer for 30 minutes, and answer the following question:

What do I want my life to look like by becoming an A-Game Player?

Spend the entire 30 minutes answering this question. Even if you think you're done after five minutes, allow yourself the whole time to contemplate and write down everything you can think of. This is a pure stream of consciousness, so don't worry about the specifics. We'll consolidate it all into a concise statement in the next step.

To help lubricate the gears, ask yourself the following questions:

What type of person do I want to become through my journey in poker?

Who are the people that I want to associate with and have strong relationships with?

What are the activities I want to do on a regular basis—think daily, weekly, semi-annually, and annually. What are the actions I absolutely don't want to do?

Set that timer and let's begin!

..

...

.....

......

All right, great job! Hopefully, you have plenty of ideas to work with. Now it's time to consolidate everything you came up with into a concise vision statement. I'm not going to give you a specific format. This is something that's just for you. Distill what you wrote down into two or three sentences. Don't worry about being perfect. Your vision statement will evolve alongside you on your journey to becoming the best version of yourself. Having this statement will allow you to look at your actions and decide if you're on the correct path to living your vision. This is the rocket fuel that will power your A-Game Engine.

Chapter 15

Scheduling for Success

If you're not doing many of the activities that are part of the A-Game Engine, you might be wondering how there is time in the day to fit it all in. While nobody can create time, everyone is allocated the same amount each day, and you have the ability to consciously choose how you spend it. There are four main areas an A-Game Player dedicates time to each day, and we build our schedule by filling them out in the following order:

- Foundational Activities (Planning, Nutrition, Fitness, Sleep)
- Recovery
- Study
- Playing Time

Invariably, when I'm working with someone and we start to make a schedule, the first thing they want to do is fill in their playing time. Obviously, playing time is incredibly important. It's how we turn poker skill into profits. And I get it. Playing is the exciting part, the part that gets our juices going. But our overarching goal is to schedule our activities with an eye toward being able to bring our A-game each time we play. To do that, we need to include all of the activities that we listed in answer to the fundamental performance question, namely, what are the best players in the world doing that I'm not?

Your schedule is how you ensure everything is in place, and once you've successfully implemented this system, I think you'll be amazed at just how much more you're able to accomplish while feeling less stress and pressure than you did when you were trying to fit in everything on the fly.

A-Game Exercise: Create Your Schedule Template

Creating a schedule can be a daunting exercise if you're starting off with a blank slate.

So, what I want you to do is get out the notebook or document you're using for these exercises, and we'll go step by step to create a template you can use as a starting point each week. Create a page for Monday, with a row for each hour of the day starting at midnight. So, 24 rows in total (even better 48 rows, with each row representing a 30-minute chunk). Then make a similar page for the other six days of the week.

If you want to skip this step, you can use the template I've created, which you can find in the resources page at:

AGamePoker.com/resources

Ready? Let's jump right in.

We'll start with foundational activities, the first of which is planning. Yes, we do need to plan to plan. If you're going to implement a schedule, you need to make time each week to lay out your schedule. This can be done in a few ways. You can build out your schedule on a day-by-day basis. (Typically, I find the most effective way is to set aside 30 minutes each evening to review the day just finished and plan for the day to come). Or you can do it on a weekly basis where you have a set time each week to plan your schedule for the following week. You can also do a combination, where you plan your schedule on a weekly basis and then have a quick review-and-adjust time at the end of each day.

I'm a big fan of the hybrid method as it gives you your major planning time once a week, which really allows you to make the most conscious choice of allocating your time but also allows you the flexibility of reviewing and adjusting on a day-to-day basis. So, choose the method you're going to use and fill in the slots allocated to this activity as Review and Planning.

The next foundational items are nutrition and fitness. An A-game player must be properly fueled, so it's important to have time on our schedule to address proper nutrition. This is especially important if you're playing longer sessions, where you may get so locked in you'll fail to meet your physical needs while playing.

Fitness is another foundational staple. Scheduling fitness in advance gives you a much higher likelihood of actually following through on it. Having an idea of what your overall fitness routine will look like and pre-planning it into your week makes this one of the first things you'll want to get down on your schedule.

Decide where you'll ideally allocate time for eating and fitness and fill them in the schedule. There are many options for food timing, you'll know what's most optimal for you. For fitness, I find that most players do well shooting for at least three hours per week. Depending on where you are in your fitness journey you may decide on more time or less. What's most important now is that you have time on your schedule dedicated to this activity.

Last but not least in foundational activities is sleep. Sleep is an essential component for all high-performers. It's true that for poker players many games will require unconventional sleep schedules, but the key aspect of scheduling is to remain consciously flexible, not rigid. That's why we want to think about our sleep schedule and have it be one of the first things we enter on our calendar.

Remember, this is your schedule template, not something you need to stick to religiously. Things will change based on circumstances. What's important is that you make any changes consciously. So, go ahead and fill out your ideal sleeping schedule for each day.

Next, we move on to scheduling recovery activities. You might be a little surprised that I'm having you fill out your recovery slots before study or playing time. However, the point of the schedule is to get in all the items that need to be checked off the list, and the foundational and the recovery items are usually the ones that are missed in lieu of playing and studying extra.

Just like professional athletes need recovery time in order to perform their best while in the field of play, so do poker players. If you saw an athlete finish a game or a match and go straight into a workout, then wake up the following morning and do another workout, pushing their body to its limits before playing another game, you'd advise them to take a step back so that they can perform at their best.

The same is true of poker, although it's not as immediately apparent in a mental competition as it is in a physical one. Yet burnout and low-level performance degradation happen for poker players, too. A-Game Poker isn't just about playing your best in a single moment or going full-out now only to burn out later, it's about consistently achieving high levels of performance and playing your best all the time. And for that to happen, we need to add recovery to our schedule.

This includes leisure activities, hobbies, and relaxation (like going to the sauna or getting a massage), and social activities with family and friends. Even stuff like video games and Netflix are perfectly acceptable recovery activities when chosen consciously. Remember, we aren't here to judge how you spend your time, we're here to make that decision consciously. Video games can be a massive distraction, or they can be a fantastic way to recover. It all just depends on how you approach them.

Many poker players, especially the most enthusiastic, feel that they can play long hours, seven days a week. That just isn't the case long term. I always recommend to my clients that they take a minimum of one day off a week. Two to three days is very common, depending upon your game. I know this area is going to be easy for you to skip if you're in a highly motivated stage, but it's essential that you make sure recovery is on the schedule before you put in your playing time.

So, the next step is to fill in slots specifically for recovery time. If you have activities you know you want to hold these slots, put them in, otherwise just mark them as Recovery. Later in this book we'll go over recovery strategies, so you'll have a better idea then which activities you want to include.

One of the hallmarks of an A-Game Player is deliberately planning study time. These are away-from-the-table activities that are designed to increase your profitability in the game. The key part when you're scheduling your skill-acquisition activities is to be deliberate about what you plan to study. It's not enough just to put "study" on the agenda and then sit down and go from there. For the same reason that we're creating a schedule in the first place, we want to be thoughtful about our plan of study.

Studying poker isn't magic. The simple act of doing it doesn't make you a better player.

To study effectively, you need to be focusing on the right area of the game with the right methods in order to get the proper results and make sure the skills you're improving can be retained long-term. How you study is one of your biggest edges in poker. Unfortunately, what most people pass off as poker study is really just a form of entertainment disguised as study. An A-Game player schedules their study, schedules how they study, schedules what to study, and does it with the objective intention of specifically improving an important area of their game.

How much time you allocate to this is going to depend on a number of factors: Where you are in your career, how tough the games you're playing in are, and whether or not you're in a season of high volume, such as a large MTT series or an incredibly profitable game that's running long hours. All these factors go into deciding how much you study. Typically, most of my clients are aiming for five to ten hours a week. Deciding this balance is another part of being an A-Game Player.

When making your schedule each week, the optimal strategy is to delineate exactly what you plan to study during each allotted time block. However, for now we'll just fill in those slots with Study, as we are just creating a rough template for you to work from in the future. Go ahead and do that now.

The last piece of the puzzle, after you've scheduled everything else, is your playing time. How you approach playing time will vary greatly by the type of game. If you're playing online cash games or other online games that have high liquidity and consistent availability, you'll be able to use that reliability to create a more conventional and consistent schedule. If you're playing online MTTs, you'll be able to have consistent start times as well as being able to schedule when you stop registering for tournaments. But obviously, you won't be able to predict when exactly your session will end. Still, as you play your schedule, you'll have a reasonable expectation of how long you'll go on average and be able to adjust accordingly. Live cash game players will be able to schedule times where the games are consistently good but will also have to be flexible enough to play in games that pop up unexpectedly. Live tournament players will have a good bit of variation, as you're usually planning around a series of events. But knowing the tournament schedules ahead of time should enable you to plan for all the different contingencies.

No matter what format you play, I suggest adding 15-30 minutes on either side for a warm-up and cool-down. I'll be providing protocols for each later in this book. To finish off this exercise go ahead and fill out your ideal playing schedule, factoring everything I mentioned above.

You now have a template for your ideal schedule! Use it as a tool to help with your daily or weekly planning. My expectation isn't that you'll be able to rigidly stick with this schedule each week. That's not the point. The point is that you consciously choose how you spend your time, and then review how you actually spend it. Remember, you can either have the freedom to do whatever you want when you want and get little done, or you can implement a schedule and accomplish *everything* you want. Now that you have a template, implementing that schedule will be much easier.

CHAPTER 16

FUEL FOR HIGH-PERFORMANCE POKER

Top poker players have acknowledged that the quality of their diet directly influences their energy levels and cognitive functions during games. This is why you see many more players arranging for delivery of chef-cooked meals at the tables instead of ordering a burger and fries off the menu. Most of the upper-echelon players treat their dietary habits with the same seriousness as professional athletes. This involves not only selecting the right foods but also understanding how what they're putting in their body impacts their energy and focus.

Implementing a performance-focused diet and nutrition plan is the definition of a freeroll. We know the impact that healthy eating has on health and longevity, so any additional EV that is gained is gravy (or maybe I should say Extra Virgin cold-pressed olive oil).

With all that said, it is possible to take your focus on diet and nutrition too far. Some players treat their dietary choices more like a religion than a performance optimization. There's no such thing as a one-size-fits-all "Perfect Poker Diet," and it is possible to do more harm than good by over-obsessing on the details of your personal nutrition plan. The reason I choose not to dive too deep into scientific research in this section is because I can find a study to "prove" nearly any position when it comes to what the optimal diet is for poker performance.

If I wanted to tell you that a vegan diet was optimal, I could find a study for that.

If I wanted to tell you that a carnivore diet was optimal, I could find a study for that. If I wanted to tell you that a diet consisting of only bananas and potatoes was optimal, I could probably find a study for that as well. The research surrounding diet and nutrition is incredibly complicated, and points to an optimal solution being more individualized than one-size-fits-all. I've had clients who have thrived on vegan diets. I've had clients who had a vegan diet completely tank their performance. The same is true for pretty much every "named" diet you can think of.

If you're hoping I'm going to share the "Perfect Poker Diet" in this book, you're going to be disappointed, because it doesn't exist. Just like everything else we've discussed in this book, optimization comes from consistent iteration. I can share this: Most of my clients land on a diet relatively balanced on macros, low on refined sugars, with minimal processed foods. Most have also found a significant benefit by limiting alcohol consumption.

Finding what works best for you requires experimentation. This involves trying different diets and foods and noting how each affects your energy levels and mental clarity. It's also crucial to be aware of any food allergies or intolerances, as these can significantly impact your health and performance. Professional guidance from a nutritionist or a dietitian can be invaluable in this journey.

For those serious about their poker career, investing in professional assistance for diet optimization can be highly beneficial. This not only simplifies the process, it takes the onus off the player in figuring out the best diet and nutrition plan. Most of us consume food somewhere between three and six times a day, and to have to think and worry about what you're eating at your next meal can burn significant mental energy that could be put to better use elsewhere.

Hiring a private chef, for instance, is not as unattainable as it might seem. The cost of a chef who can shop, prepare, and cook all your meals is much less than you might expect, especially if you compare it to ordering out every meal. There are also countless meal delivery services tailored to every possible diet and delivered to your door on a regular basis, requiring only that you spend a few minutes heating them up in the comfort of your kitchen. This investment not only ensures healthy eating but also frees up significant time for poker preparation, performance, and recovery. For those not ready to hire a chef or use a meal delivery service, batch cooking is a practical alternative. Preparing healthy meals for the week or even the entire month can save time and ensure you always have nutritious food at hand. This approach allows you to focus more on your game and less on daily meal preparations.

There's no universal "perfect" diet for poker players, but there is an ideal diet for you. Discovering this requires experimentation, awareness, and sometimes professional guidance. The effort you put into optimizing your diet is an investment in your poker career, promising not just better health but also a sharper mind and improved performance at the table.

A-Game Exercise: Nutrition Assessment

When it comes to nutrition, there are three key questions to ask yourself:

Is my nutrition plan optimizing performance in the short term?

Is my nutrition plan optimizing my long-term performance and lifespan?

Is my nutrition plan minimizing the amount of time I need to be thinking about food choices?

Take some time to answer each of these questions, then come up with one action step for each of the three areas. For the short term, maybe you start to experiment with finding your optimal pre-session meal, or preparing small snacks to maintain your energy throughout your session. For the long term, maybe it's researching the nutritional strategies that have the most evidence for supporting longevity. For minimizing time, maybe you research hiring a private chef in your area, research meal plan options, or devise a meal-prep system.

CHAPTER 17

EXCELLENCE THROUGH EXERCISE

I'm sure you'll hear, even to this day, the argument that because poker is not a physical game, physical fitness has little bearing on results. But when you look at what the best players in the world are doing, it becomes clear that *they* believe that it does, which is why many put such a high level of emphasis on this area.

If you only follow one piece of advice in this book, it should be to implement a fitness routine into your life starting immediately. Heightened mental acuity, increased focus, enhanced memory, reduced stress levels, all these are regularly reported performance benefits associated with physical fitness.

Let's focus on the specific benefits of fitness for a poker player.Improved concentration and mental endurance are paramount in poker, where games can last for hours and the smallest lapse in attention can cost you dearly. Regular exercise has been shown to sharpen focus and extend the duration for which you can maintain peak mental performance. This is not just beneficial for poker; it's a life-enhancing change.

Moreover, stress management is a critical aspect of poker. The game's inherent uncertainties and high stakes can lead to significant stress, which can, in turn, impair decision-making. Exercise–especially aerobic activities like running, swimming, or even brisk walking–is a proven stress buster. It releases endorphins, the body's natural mood lifters, helping you maintain a calm and composed demeanor at the table.

What about memory? Remembering your opponents' playing styles, recalling past hands, and keeping track of betting patterns are vital skills in poker. Regular physical activity, particularly cardiovascular exercises, has been linked to improved memory and cognitive function. This isn't just beneficial for your poker game; it's a long-term investment in your overall mental health.

In addition to these direct benefits, there's also the aspect of self-discipline. Establishing and maintaining a regular fitness regime requires discipline, a trait that is invaluable at the poker table. The self-control and routines you develop through exercise often translate into better decision-making and greater emotional control during games.

Let's not forget the health benefits. Poker is a sedentary activity. Regular exercise counters these risks, promoting cardiovascular health, better sleep patterns, and overall well-being. Finally, there are undeniable perks that come with being more physically attractive.

You might wonder, if fitness is so beneficial, why isn't everyone doing it? I'm guessing you've heard everything I'm saying here and that it's not news to you. The fact is, if the benefits of exercise were put into a pill that you could buy, it would be the best-selling pill on the market, hands down. So why is it so hard for most people to make exercise a consistent part of their life? Because exercise is hard work. Exercise demands that you work hard with no visible or immediate reward, it requires adjusting your mindset. It requires understanding that as your body gets acclimated to the work and starts to crave the hormones and neurochemicals that are released post-exercise, the rewards will become tangible. The challenge is sticking with it long enough to form the habit and reap these benefits.

Later in this book you'll learn about the negative subconscious programs that I call Detrimental Mental Programs. Beyond the typical activation energy it takes to get a fitness routine started, these programs can throw up a mental roadblock, halting your progress in its tracks.

If you want to become an A-Game Player, you can't afford to ignore your fitness. It's not just about looking good; it's about honing your mental edge, managing stress, and building the discipline that translates into success at the table and in life.

A-Game Exercise: Minimum Acceptable Exercise

Your exercise for this chapter is to exercise. I want you to take a few moments and plan a minimum amount of time you can devote to your physical fitness. Many people avoid getting started on their fitness because they think it's not worth it if they don't go big from the start.

If you're new to regular exercise, even something as simple as five push-ups a day, or a 10-minute walk can be a starting point. Add a few more each week, and gradually, you'll build a sustainable routine. The goal is consistent, gradual progress, not an unsustainable burst of activity.Choosing the right exercise routine is critical, and it must align with your personal drives and lifestyle.

What motivates you? What kind of physical activity might you enjoy? The answers to these questions are crucial. This is where understanding your vision and drives, as we discussed earlier in the book, becomes invaluable. By aligning your fitness regime with your personal goals and preferences, you significantly increase the likelihood of it becoming a permanent part of your life.

Just as with diet and nutrition, I advise those with sufficient resources to outsource their fitness routines by hiring a personal trainer. Doing this allows you to save all the mental bandwidth that comes with planning and developing a routine, as well as giving you the built-in accountability to someone other than yourself, who will help you maintain the habit.

Remember, the best players aren't just skilled with cards; they are complete individuals who understand the importance of a balanced, healthy lifestyle. So, start small, stay consistent, and watch as your game–and your life–transforms.

CHAPTER 18

SCALING YOUR SKILLS

Technical skill is the cornerstone of success in poker. An A-Game Player cannot compensate for deficient technical skills through some sort of magical mental game power that allows them to be successful regardless.

An A-Game Player is someone who maximizes their earnings with the skills that they already have. An A-Game Player also recognizes that, by raising the ceiling of their skills, their profit potential will skyrocket. The more skill you have the more opportunities for profit exist.

The most skilled player in the world could neglect much of what we discuss in the book and still achieve relatively high levels of success. Of course, if they also followed the A-Game System they would be even better—an unstoppable force in the world of poker.

The way that players look to improve their technical skills has evolved alongside advances in the game. In fact, it's the methodology and tools of skill acquisition that have caused the biggest shifts in poker over the years. From intuition and experience to real-time AI powered GTO trainers, the way players approach skill acquisition has changed massively.

The skill of improving your skill is just as important as the skill of applying your skill. As the game has progressed, and the tools for skill acquisition have evolved, the roles of poker student and poker player have become more disparate. For players in past eras, skill acquisition took place on the fly. The best players were the ones who could adapt their in-game experience and synthesize it to increase skill as they played. But by this point, every serious poker player understands how important off-the-table study is to long-term success. Very few players, however, take an optimized approach to improvement. In previous eras you would gain a big advantage simply by being someone who studied a modest 5-10 hours a week. Many players spent much less time than that, if they studied at all.

The goal of this chapter is to show you it's not only the fact that you study that matters, it's how and what you study. In an era where all serious players are putting in an optimal number of hours studying the game, the ones who make the most progress in those hours gain a massive advantage. In other words, all study time is not created equal. Studying inefficiently may not only fail to improve your skills, it can actually lead to your play getting worse. The fact is, it's easier to make no progress than it is to make meaningful gains.

Obviously, it's easier and more fun to throw on a training video, a Twitch stream, or a high-stakes live cash game than it is to pull thousands of hands from a spot you think you may be leaking, run them through a simulator, come up with a new strategy, and then devise a practice plan dedicated to training for that specific spot. Players refer to both of these kinds of activities as study, but only one makes you a better player.

In today's game, the player who improves their skill in the most directed and efficient way gains an insurmountable edge over their competition.

That's because gains in skill compound. If Player A and B start at the same skill level, and Player A improves even 10%

more per hour of study, Player B will quickly be left in Player A's dust. Rate of acquired skill is one of the biggest opportunities in today's game. There have never been more tools at your disposal than there are now, and that statement will hold true no matter when you read this book. The bottleneck to improving skill is no longer access to knowledge but your ability to synthesize and incorporate the available knowledge into skill.

I am not a technical poker coach. You will not learn any technical poker skills from me. What I can teach you is a framework of how to approach your study in a way that rapidly levels up your game, a framework that you can then apply to the resources you have available. The first thing I want to discuss is what it actually means to study the game.

This is going to be a huge shift for the majority of you, because this is where most poker players go wrong. Not understanding how to approach study means that you're putting in the study hours but getting little to no return on your investment of time. So, here's my definition of poker study:

A process for acquiring and improving your poker skills.

Unfortunately, the way most players approach the game helps little in the way of "acquisition" and does even less in the area of "improvement."

The Three Stages of Study

My clients have found the most success by breaking study into three distinct stages, all of which serve the overall goal of increasing skill. There's the Acquire stage, there's the Review stage, and finally the Practice stage.

The Acquire stage is learning, gaining, and adding skills that you didn't have previously. Put simply, it's learning new concepts that you didn't know before. So, whether you're consuming a new theory video, going through a new course, reading a new book or discussing a new concept with a coach, you're in the Acquire stage. Obviously, it's important to learn new skills, but it's a problem if you spend all your time doing that while ignoring the other two stages. The truth is, not only does learning a new skill not guarantee an immediate improvement in your win rate, it sometimes actually has the opposite effect. Because when you learn a new strategy, applying it can be difficult at first. Often, it can lead to short-term results that are no better or even worse than what you were producing before. If that's true for one skill, think of what happens when you're constantly consuming new material, and spending little time Reviewing or Practicing. It can lead to a situation where someone may sound like they're a good player, but the reality is that their knowledge only runs surface deep.

If all you're doing is consuming, consuming, consuming every new piece of content you find, then you'll struggle to apply it at the table, which is the ultimate end goal of acquiring poker skill. To gain a deep understanding and have it translate to applicable skill, you need to continually review and practice. Players who are imbalanced in Acquire, feel like they're working. They'll often wonder how they can be putting in so much effort without seeing a tangible increase in their results. They read every new poker book, know exactly what time each training site drops their weekly videos, and are the first to purchase new courses when they're released. But when it's just new concept after new concept there's no space in which to become proficient let alone master any of them.

The second stage is Review. This is taking concepts that you know, and going over them again and again in order to understand them at a deeper level and be able to integrate them into your skill set. This can consist of asking questions of a coach, going over a theory video with a group of your peers, or rereading/rewatching poker content and taking notes as a way to embed that knowledge deep into your subconscious. This stage is also about taking concepts that you already know and reinforcing them by consciously gaining a better understanding of them.

Finally, we have stage three, Practice. Practice is taking a skill you already have and drilling it over and over again to take it from intellectual understanding to actual implementation. There's a big gap between simply knowing something and having mastery over its application.

You improve your ability to apply a skill by practicing in a focused, deliberate manner. You take action, get feedback, adjust and repeat. This type of practice is common for athletes, but is rare in the poker world. For most poker players the only thing that comes close to deliberate practice and drills is playing a session and reviewing hands after. This is something that most poker players literally never do off the table. Someone who spends time deliberately practicing vital skills nearly everyday, is someone who is on the path to mastery. Here are some examples:

If you're trying to study a specific leak and you isolate that leak in your database and look at all the hands that fit the situation and then work the situation over and over again—that would be a form of drilling.

If you're practicing opening ranges, a simple way to drill is to have a chart that shows those opening ranges in a specific scenario, after which you can go through all your recent hands and compare them to the chart. Assuming that it's an accurate chart, it will be an instant feedback mechanism that can help you improve this skill rapidly.

The more you drill a particular skill, the more competent you'll become, until eventually you'll master it to the point where it will become reflex. Which is another way of saying that once you've mastered the opening charts, they'll become an unconscious part of your game. In turn, that will make your in-game play more efficient because you won't have to spend energy thinking about your decisions in that specific spot.

So, that's the three stages. Acquire, Review and Practice. As a quick thought exercise before we move on. Take a moment to estimate what percent of your study time you devote to each of the three stages.

What percentage do you spend on Acquire?

What percentage do you spend on Review?

What percentage do you spend on Practice?

Now that we understand the Three Stages of Study, the next question is: *How do we use this framework to become better at the game?* The truth is, most players will study aimlessly, even very good players.

Study for most players consists of opening up a few training sites, seeing which one has the most recent video, then putting it on in the background while they bumble around in forums and social media. Believe it or not, more than a few of the live players that I've worked with will tell me that all the study they do is watch high-stakes poker TV shows. Now, let's be honest. Neither of those activities really even count as study; it's more like entertainment. Passively watching a video on a new concept is in the realm of "Acquisition" but doesn't actually count as you won't retain any of that knowledge by using this approach. Unless you're specifically planning to play against the players featured in a particular TV show and using the footage to pick up tendencies, there is likely very little that you'll be able to translate from a show like this into your own game.

Now, maybe you're already taking a better approach than this to your study. Maybe you're saving hands from your sessions or reviewing them later, either by running them through software or discussing them with your peers, or both. Perhaps you're already watching training videos in a deliberate manner, taking notes and formulating questions about concepts you're not quite sure about. Maybe you're even doing a bit of drilling when it comes to learning opening range charts or other specific scenarios. If you're already taking a more thoughtful approach to how you study, it might be the case that you're not being so thoughtful about *what* you study.

Here's the thing with poker. There are thousands and thousands of situations you can study, but most people just jump between them randomly. Maybe you found a situation that was interesting, so you devoted the next few hours to figuring it out. Maybe you watched a really good training video and spent the next week running simulations to get a good grasp on the scenario that was discussed. While doing that isn't a complete waste of time, and certainly better than doing nothing, it neglects one key question:

What can I study today that will earn me the greatest ROI over the long run?

Remember, study is an investment of time. There are lots of things that you could study, but many fewer that you *should be* studying. What you choose to study, and how you approach that time, will have a massive impact on the return you get from that investment. So while you're deciding on where to start, we go back to the essential question:

What can I study today that will earn me the greatest ROI over the long run?

For most people, even those of you at the higher stakes, the answer to that question is "the fundamentals." One of my favorite books of all time is The Art of Learning by Josh Waitzkin. A quote from that book sums up this point better than I ever could:

"The fact is, when there is intense competition, those who succeed have slightly more honed skills than the rest. It's rarely a mysterious technique that drives us to the top but rather a profound mastery of what may well be the basic skill set. Depth beats breadth any day of the week because it opens a channel for the intangible, unconscious, creative components of our hidden potential."

Let me repeat the most important part of that quote, just to drive it home:

"It's rarely a mysterious technique that drives us to the top but rather a profound mastery of what may well be the basic skill set."

In poker terms, this is the difference between studying a river check-raise spot from a tricky opponent versus drilling opening ranges and other preflop scenarios. One situation, you might go months or years before encountering again, the other happens literally every hand.

When you take a scattershot approach, you may end up spending a lot of time studying, but the value you get may be little to none. When you put your emphasis on mastering the fundamentals, you drastically reduce the time it takes to level up your game.

If you were to spend the next six months figuring out what the fundamentals of your game are (Acquire) and found the best resources covering this area (Review), then spent the majority of your study time drilling them (Practice), you would put yourself so far ahead of the curve that you'd achieve a level that would take most players years to accomplish, if they ever did at all.

In previous eras, the fact that you spent any significant amount of time thinking about the game away from the table was sufficient for those with an above average intelligence and natural inclination towards the game. In the modern game, that level of effort will get you left behind. An A-Game player works to understand the most profitable areas of the game to study, then implements a blueprint for rapidly improving that area of their game.

Think back to the exercise we did earlier, where you noted the percentage of time you spent in each of the three stages. If Practice did not claim the majority stake of your time, the fastest way to improve is to adjust until practice is roughly in the 50-80% range. Once you feel you've hit a plateau you can divert more of your attention to Acquisition, but remember that the goal of study is to raise the ceiling of the skill we're able to apply on the table, and Practice is the main tool we use to accomplish that goal.

Training sites, courses, study groups, and coaches mean that the knowledge of what spots to study is no longer a major barrier to success. Further, many of the modern training tools have made drilling specific spots much easier and accessible. When you combine those resources with the framework discussed here, you have everything you need to get the most return out of the time you invest in studying the game.

A-Game Exercise: Analyze Your Approach

Where you start depends entirely on where you're at in the game currently. A player new to the game will need to approach study in a completely different way than a 15-year veteran.

For this A-Game exercise, I want you to spend some time writing out how you currently approach study. Estimate what percentage of your time you spend in each stage, and then be brutally honest with what your current study approach looks like. Next, take some time to analyze your approach, and based on what you've learned so far, take some time to list ways you can improve your approach. Finally, come up with three areas of the game you think will have the greatest impact on your results, and come up with a rough plan on how you can use the three-phase approach to improve in those areas.

Congratulations, you've now put in more thought into the structure of your study than most players ever will. Of course, A-Game Players are not other players and you'll use this momentum to increase your skill at a rate much faster than your competition.

CHAPTER 19

THE PERFORMANCE PHASE

As we delve into the Performance Phase of the A-Game Poker System, it's crucial to grasp what "Performance" truly means. Performance, in its simplest definition, is:

The act of accomplishing a task or function.

However, in the context of poker, this definition is too rudimentary. Performance here isn't just about taking action; it's about the quality of those actions and how they measure up against your highest potential.

Consider your gameplay in terms of your A, B, or C Game. This isn't a comparison to others but a reflection of your own personal skill set. Here, we focus on Efficiency, a term we covered in the "6 Levers Of Poker Profits" section. Efficiency is the percentage of time you're applying the full extent of your skill while playing. At your absolute best, your play is at a level of 100; for the purposes of ranking your play, let's say that your A-Game range is 90 to 100, your B-Game 75 to 89, and your C-Game 50 to 74. While these aren't measurable levels in real-time, they serve as a framework: You aim for the 90-100 range and recognize when you fall below that level. It's a battle of Potential Skill vs Applied Skill.

How do we narrow the gap between potential and application? To excel in poker, we must identify and optimize key performance factors. Performance in poker hinges on two main aspects: information gathering and decision making.

In the context of potential versus applied skill, there are two main factors that contribute to optimal decision making: emotions and energy. As we will cover in the section on tilt, emotions have a massive influence on decisions. The same is true for energy, which is why we put an emphasis on nutrition, fitness, sleep, and recovery. You'll also find the A-Game Audit later in this section, an in-game tool I've provided, which in part is designed to help you monitor your energy.

The more information you have, the more you'll be able to apply your skill in decision making. Poker, inherently a game of incomplete information, demands keen data collection. Every poker decision, whether consciously calculated or not, is a mathematical equation. The more information you possess, the better you can solve that equation.

Remember the Ultimate Bet and Absolute Poker superuser scandals in the early 2000s? They demonstrated the power of information. Conversely, imagine playing poker blindfolded and with noise-blocking headphones, only removing them briefly for your turn. The lack of information and processing time would be a significant disadvantage.

Our ability to gather the best information we're capable of gathering, comes down to attention. The skill of directing our attention is called focus. In the blindfold example I gave a moment ago, our attention was artificially restricted, meaning we were not able to gather information. While you'll unlikely never encounter a situation as extreme as that example, there are endless ways your attention can be pulled away from the game while playing. With the state of technology this has never been more true, and the battle will only become increasingly fierce as we progress further. In my A-Game Poker Masterclass I devote most of a module to the topic, with exercises designed specifically to build up your focus muscles.

Owning this book makes you eligible for a significant discount on the course. Learn more in the resource section: AGamePoker.com/resources

In the next chapter I'll share one of the most powerful tools I've developed to lock in focus before your session, the A.G.A.M.E. Pre-Session Protocol.

PRO CASE STUDY

BRIAN RAST

2023 POKER HALL OF FAME INDUCTEE WITH OVER $25,000,000 IN LIVE TOURNAMENT EARNINGS

When I started working with Elliot in 2015, I was beginning to get my footing in the big game in Bobby's Room. Coming from a big-bet background, I had a lot of work to do on the limit games in the mix, especially the up-card games. The dynamic in these games is much different than in flop games, as so much more information is available. To excel at these games, you need to collect and retain that information to factor into your decision-making later in the hand.

Even though I was playing for massive stakes against some of the most seasoned players at these games, I would catch myself deep in hands, having not tracked any of the up cards, doing stuff like watching a basketball game instead. It was evident that I had a significant focus deficit, and if I was going to beat these games, I had to fix it.

I was initially skeptical about the hypnosis and visualization side of Elliot's work. I quickly realized that my preconceptions were wrong. All it is, is a form of suggestive meditation where I relax deeply, and my brain and subconscious are more accepting of the ideas we're trying to implement. And when the time comes to perform, those ideas happen without much conscious effort.

It was very effective and immediately impacted my results in the game. It's been my experience that you gain a significant edge by increasing the percentage of time you play to your full capabilities; call it your A-Game vs. your B- or C-Game. Having max focus and concentration is necessary to play your true A-Game, and it does require a lot of effort and mental energy. Being in the right mindset to do that over many hours is difficult.

I've found the visualization strategies I've worked on with Elliot to be a highly effective way to unlock that part of my game. They are not making me a better player, but they make it easier to access my ability to perform up to my full capabilities more frequently.

CHAPTER 20

THE A.G.A.M.E. PRE-SESSION PROTOCOL

As you can see in the A-Game Engine graphic, the transition from Preparation to Performance is the A.G.A.M.E. Pre-Session Protocol. Now, before we get into the exact steps, let's make sure we understand exactly why it's so important to install this transitional step into your game. I've had many clients, who scoff at the idea of spending 20-30 minutes before a session to prepare, rapidly change their minds and end up swearing by the system once they give it a try.

The truth is, a poker session is a high-performance event, and it requires a different mindset and deeper focus than other activities in your life. Most players do not make this distinction. They never take the time to prepare their mind to perform and intentionally lock in their focus. But like we always say, A-Game Players aren't most players.

When you study elite performers, from professional athletes to chess grandmasters, even Hollywood actors, the overwhelming majority have pre-game rituals that help them get ready to perform. If an athlete has a match at 7 pm, you never see them arrive at 6:45 and jump straight onto the field. Most of them are there a minimum of three hours early, to go over strategy and prepare their minds and bodies for performance. Rather than hit the field cold and just hope they can instantly switch into performance mode, they carefully craft specific routines to get themselves mentally and physically ready for the start of a match. These elite performers can't afford to leave their performance to chance, and if you want to consistently play your A-Game and bring the best version of yourself each time you play, then neither can you.

The option is between starting cold with the hope you'll perform well, and installing a routine that gets you there nearly every time. As an A-Game Player, I think I know which option you'll choose.

The good news is, you won't need anything close to the three hours plus that a professional athlete needs to prepare, the A.G.A.M.E. Pre-session Protocol can be done in just 20 to 30 minutes. The aim of a pre-session routine is to be the bridge that separates performance time from the rest of your life, the transition from preparation to performance.

Your goal is to eliminate distractions and compartmentalize this time from any outside stress, worries, thoughts or emotions. To set your focus on what you need to do to be successful and adjust the challenge level to optimize that focus. To prepare your mind for high levels of focus and entry into "The Zone." We do this through 5 simple steps:

A: Attend to Physical Needs

G: Goals for the session

A: Activate Your Mind

M: Mindset MP3 or Meditation

E: Eliminate all distractions.

Attend To Physical Needs

In the first step, *Attend to Physical Needs*, we ensure that your body is prepared to serve your mind. This means having a supply of nutritious snacks and water on hand, making sure to wear the proper clothing that gives you the flexibility to adjust to changes in temperature, so you won't be too hot or too cold.

You'll also want to make sure you go to the bathroom before sitting down to play. It's amazing how many people skip the bathroom step and completely lose focus when they have to use the restroom a few minutes into their session.

The point here is to give your body everything it needs, so that physical needs or discomforts don't become a distraction while you're playing. If you haven't done some light exercise earlier in the day, you can also throw in a quick bit of exercise to give yourself that extra boost of focus and mental performance.

Goals For the Session

This is where you intentionally set your focus and challenge level for the session. Go over strategic goals and possible challenges for your session. Setting specific intentions for areas of your game you want to focus on and controlling your level of challenge during a session is a great way to ensure you're reinforcing what you need to do to be successful. This helps you hold your focus longer and gives you a better chance of getting into a flow state.

This should take 5 minutes or less.

Activate Your Mind

Here we start to transition your mind from the preparation phase over to performance. Pull up a few hands to go over so you can prepare your mind for poker. It's even better if these hands relate to the areas of focus you set in the previous step.

These can be hands from your database or hands you've saved on your computer or phone, using many of the AI solver tools available; or maybe they're simply a visualization of some specific situations. The aim is to get your mind focused on making poker decisions before any money is actually on the line. Think of this as your "warm up set" before a very heavy bench press.

This should take around 5 minutes.

MP3 or Meditation

This is the secret sauce that really separates this protocol from other methods of warming up. My pre-session MP3s are carefully crafted visualizations that are designed to clear your mind and complete the transition from preparation to performance. They're designed to lock in your focus and help you generate the mindset needed to enter into the zone and play your A-game for your entire session.

The best part is, all you have to do is put on your headphones, close your eyes, and allow me to guide you into a state of peak performance. Allow around 15 minutes for this step.

I have MP3s ranging from 6 to 20 minutes and have found the 12- to 15-minute mark to be the optimal length to get the job done. If you don't happen to have any of my MP3s on hand, you can substitute in some self-guided meditation or breathing exercises. However, as my MP3s are specifically crafted for high-performance poker, it's optimal to use them.

All readers of the book are eligible to download a free version of my Poker Pre-Game Warm Up page found on the resources page of AGamepoker.com/resources.

You'll also find a special offer and free trial of my Primed Mind app, which includes 30+ poker audios as well as hundreds of other Primers designed to help you perform your best in all areas of life.

Eliminate Distractions

In the final step, you'll want to ruthlessly eliminate distractions that could disrupt your concentration. Shut off your cell phone, ask your friends and family members to respect your time and only interrupt you if it's an emergency. Close out all your social media channels and any other unnecessary websites. This is your time to perform, your time to focus and place your full attention on the game. You've put in a lot of work to make it to this point, so please give yourself the respect you deserve and eliminate any obstacle that might impede your chances of performing at your best.

If you've done the work to prep your environment beforehand, this should only take 2-3 minutes.

Primed To Perform

You're now officially primed to perform your best. When you implement this routine before your sessions, you'll go from hoping that you'll perform well to controlling as many variables of your performance as possible, making high-performance a consistent habit. I have many clients who were hesitant and told me that it's been the most transformational change they've made, and they were able to see a massive increase in their focus and consistency once they implemented the protocol. Now it's your turn to do the same, and I'm excited to see the results you get.

One quick note, if you play multiple sessions per day: I am often asked if you should implement this routine before each session, or just before the first session of the day. My answer to that is always "it depends". If you play a session, take a short break, then play again, you're probably okay doing a modified version and running through all the steps in just 5 minutes or so. Ideally, if you have a much longer break in between sessions, you'll run through it again, or at least use one of the Mindset MP3s before your next session.

A-Game Exercise: Implement A.G.A.M.E.

For this exercise we are going to field test the A.G.A.M.E. Pre-Session Protocol. I want you to commit to using it for your next three sessions, and then after you complete your session, immediately come back to your notebook or digital document, and note any changes you noticed.

Did you feel more focused? Were you able to play your A-Game for longer? What else did you notice about how you approached the session after implementing the protocol?

Please do this as soon as you finish the session, as you'll just be guessing if you wait a few hours or days to fill this out.

The vast majority of my clients find immense benefits from implementing a warm up, and the positive reinforcement you get from writing down these benefits will help turn the protocol into a habit you use each time you play.

CHAPTER 21

THE A-GAME AUDIT

The A-Game Audit is a great way to check in on your game, so you can make a rational decision about whether you should continue playing or come back another day. The audit is a list of ten key questions you need to ask yourself to create a clear picture about the state of your game. In the final two questions, you decide whether to stop or continue, and if you decide to continue (or are forced to continue playing if you're in a tournament), see what you need to do to get back on your A-Game for the rest of your session.

On the resources page for the book, I've included a few different versions of the Audit Checklist. Which you can access at AGamePoker.com/resources.

A full-page version that you can pin-up at your workstation, as well as a business card version that's printable directly on business card stock. This way you can always have it on hand when you need it.

There are two main times when an A-Game Audit is most beneficial. First, as a regularly scheduled part of your playing routine. Just as you should plan breaks, you should plan A-Game Audits. In fact, you can often pair these together, scheduling an audit for a few minutes before a planned break.

If you have more infrequent breaks, you might want to schedule this a bit more often. Something like once an hour works great for many people. If you play very long sessions, you can also start to increase the frequency of your audits the longer you play. If you're playing an 8-hour session maybe you start with every two hours, and by the end be checking in with yourself every 30 minutes.

This reminder helps you stay focused on what's important and helps you to actively cultivate the ideal mindset for playing your A-Game. You can either use an alarm on your phone to set check-in times, or an alarm on a watch or even a kitchen egg timer, if you're playing online. You can use environmental cues as well, such as time on the tournament clock, or base it around dealer changes. Pretty much anything that happens in regular intervals can be used as a cue.

Another opportunity to use the audit is in moments when you feel triggered. If you notice a rapid shift in your emotional state, the A-Game Audit can be a quick way to get yourself back on the right track or get you off the tracks completely if you discover you're headed directly for a cliff.

The act of asking yourself these 10 questions might be enough to give you necessary perspective on destructive emotions and prevent you from veering off into emotional (and poor) decision making.

So, a quick recap of what we covered so far: The A-Game Audit is a 30-second mental checklist to see what level you're playing at. You should plan A-Game audits at various points throughout your sessions, possibly slotting them in just before you take a break.

You should also use them if you feel emotionally triggered, or through any other cue you've discovered that leads you to playing anything less than your A-Game. Here's the full of the checklist points one by one:

Are You Playing on Auto Pilot?

If the answer is yes, you're in the danger zone. Either something needs to change quickly, or it's time to wrap the session up soon. Sometimes just noticing you're on autopilot is enough to switch it off, but oftentimes once you hit this point it means your energy is depleted and it's either time to take a break or it's time to call it a session.

Obviously, the end goal is to be able to get back on track if you notice yourself going on autopilot. You just need to be honest with yourself about whether or not that's possible in the moment.

What's Your Focus Level (1-10)

Give yourself a quick focus rating to see where you're at.

If the answer to autopiloting is yes, you're going to be in the 1-3 range for sure. If you're at an 8-plus, that's great news, anything lower, you'll need to be cautious going forward. Once again, sometimes just realizing you're at a 5 is enough to bump you up to an 8, but make sure to factor this number into your final decision to continue playing or not.

What Letter Grade Level Are You Currently Playing At?

Grade your current game by letter grade level. So, A-Game, B-Game, C-Game, and so forth.

If you're on your A-Game that's great news, keep it going. If you're not, you'll have some things to think about as you continue on through the assessment.

What Is Your Energy Level (1-10)

Obviously, energy level is vital for being able to sustain your A-Game, so if your energy level is dipping that might be a sign you need to take a break or quit your session, even if you're currently playing great. The goal is to be aware of your energy level, and step in before a lack of energy starts to have a negative impact on your play.

How Are You Talking to Yourself?

Self-talk is vital to a proper mindset. You can often find yourself slipping into negative self-talk patterns without even realizing it. If you catch yourself doing so, that's sometimes enough to fix the issue. If not, then you might want to consider packing it in for the day or make another adjustment.

What Are You Feeling?

What emotions are going through your head at this moment? How did you react to a big hand you just lost or a massive pot you just took down? Understanding your emotional state in the moment, gives you the insight you need to make good decisions going forward.

How Do You Want to Feel?

In the last question we discovered how you are feeling, now we need to decide how you want to feel. Is how you're feeling different than how you want to be feeling? If so, then what do you need to do to make that shift?

Rate Your Current Profitability in This Game?

This is the main question you must ask yourself when determining whether to quit or continue: Is this game profitable for me?

If it's a good game, but your level of play does not make you profitable, well, you either need to get back on your A-Game or quit for the day. Or maybe your energy is very low, but your opponents' energy is even worse, making the game still quite profitable, even if you're not at your best. Or maybe you're quite profitable still, but your energy is tapped. You know you can make money at this moment, but it will have a negative impact down the road.

Rating your profitability is very important for the ninth question, which is:

Will You Continue Playing?

This checklist is not about handing you a Yes or No answer, it's about giving you the data you need to make the best decision possible, as well as a window of clarity in which to make it.

Unfortunately, I'm not able to sit behind you and make these decisions for you, and the audit itself won't make the decision for you either. What I can give you is a powerful tool to gather the pertinent information, so that you can use sound decision making when the time comes. Once you get to this point in the audit you should have all the data you need to make the best decision for your specific situation. Then, it's up to you to execute it.

Now, obviously if you're in an MTT you can't just choose to stop playing. Well, I guess you could but that would just be flushing your buy-in down the drain. If you're an online player you can decide to stop registering early, if you're not playing at a level that meets your expectations. That certainly doesn't make this tool useless. Having this information is certainly much better than not having it, even if you can't decide to stop playing.

That leads us to our final question, which is:

What Must You Do to Continue Playing at the Same Level or Higher Between Now and Your Next A-Game Audit?

If you got through the audit and everything seems great? Wonderful.

What do you need to do to maintain that level between audits? Even if things are going well now, that doesn't mean that they can't change fast. Keeping your goals and focus in mind, is a great way to keep the engine running full steam ahead.

Now, if you've decided to continue playing, but aren't on your A-Game, you must figure out what needs to change to get there, or at least to a level that maintains your minimum acceptable profitability.

This is what separates A-Game Players from the rest of the poker world. Being able to shift from C-Game To A-Game is not an easy task, but with the lessons you've learned in this book, you have the tools in your arsenal.

And there you have it, the A-Game Audit. You have the printouts, the pin-up sheet, and the business card. Put those in a place you can easily access them, so you have this tool at your fingertips when you need it. Plan regular mental check-ins and use the audit as a way to manage emotionally triggering situations.

A-Game Exercise: Audit The Audit

For this A-Game exercise, I want you to take a similar approach to when you started to implement the A.G.A.M.E. Pre-Session Protocol. The most important part is that I don't want you to implement them both at the same time. I know it can be exciting to learn a new tactic and want to immediately jump in and do it all at once. However, that's a recipe for disaster.

If you're just beginning a fitness routine and your trainer starts you off with intense max-effort interval training, followed by a complicated weight-training routine, it'd be clear they aren't very good at their job.

If you try to implement everything in this book all at once, you'll quickly get overwhelmed, and the chance that anything sticks will be slim to none.

So, *after* you've completed the A.G.A.M.E. exercise, implement the Audit into your game, and for at least three sessions, do a detailed writeup about how it impacted your play in your notebook or document.

CHAPTER 22

THE TRUTH ABOUT TILT

In A-Game Poker we talk a lot about how each hand is a puzzle or equation for you to solve, which is certainly true and an important mindset to have. At the end of the day, it's also a game of people, which means it's a game of emotions. If you don't understand the emotions of poker, both in your opponents and in yourself, then you're missing a big piece of the puzzle, a major chunk of the information needed to solve the equation.

When people come into A-Game Poker, it's tempting to try to ignore emotions all together, and to take a purely logical and analytical approach to the game. Some try to turn themselves into emotionless robots and beat themselves up whenever they have feelings. That's faulty thinking for two reasons.

First, when you try to ignore your own emotions, you tend to ignore the emotions of those around you. So, even if you were able to completely shut off your emotions, your opponents won't be doing that anytime soon. Empathy, the ability to step inside your opponent's shoes and see the world as they do, is a powerful tool for gaining information on how they play.

If you suppress, rather than take the time to understand your own emotions, you'll have a difficult time understanding the emotions of others.

Second, suppressing emotions doesn't fall in line with the aim of A-Game Poker. Remember this definition:

A system for optimizing your poker profits in a way that achieves your vision.

So, even if becoming completely emotionless was the ideal way to optimize profits, which I've just shown that it's not, then chances are it's still not something that serves your life's vision. I've yet to meet anyone whose vision is to live a life free of emotion. Rather than try to become emotionless, the A-Game Player learns to control their emotions, and more accurately, control their reactions to their emotions. Suppression is not sustainable, and poker players who try to suppress are usually those who have a massive blow up, one that's potentially career ending, after months or even years of everything seemingly being fine.

If suppression is on one end of the spectrum, submission is on the other. That's where you allow your emotions to be the driver of your decisions. This is what I call emotional decision-making, something you likely know as tilt. We'll get to that definition in a moment, but first a cautionary tale...

In the poker world, tilt is often a joke. The classic example being a Phil Hellmuth tirade where he berates his opponents, flips over a chair, and storms out of the room. Most poker players have a story either about themselves or someone they know, breaking computers, punching a wall, or doing something equally foolish. And while it might be amusing to watch Phil Hellmuth act like a juvenile, tilt is no laughing matter.

When I first came into the poker world, I remember reading a thread on an online forum about a player who had the worst instance of tilt I've ever heard of. The story went something like this:

The player described being on a multi-month downswing and, after another terrible session, threw his mouse into the wall and started punching their laptop. He mentioned that this childlike tantrum usually helped him feel better, but not this time.

Sitting on his desk was a pocket knife, which he promptly jammed deep into his ankle. He mentioned that it went in all the way to the hilt, and he went on to post pictures of his blood-soaked apartment.

Thankfully he survived, and hopefully he had the presence of mind to seek professional help. I've had clients tell me they smashed their computer screens on purpose because they were tilting so badly at the table that it was actually cheaper to smash their computer than it was to continue playing poker.

To put this in perspective, imagine this behavior in any other professional industry. Imagine you're a stock trader and you've faced some losses, and you've decided to go crazy and gamble all your investor's money away. Or imagine you're upset, and you're working in an office, and you start hitting the desk, throwing your computer around, shouting and smashing things. Probably wouldn't stay employed for very long.

The point is, this is unacceptable behavior in almost every other part of society, and if you're an extreme tilter like this, it's not something you should accept in yourself, it's certainly not how an A-Game Player behaves.

Now you might be saying "Yeah, Elliot that's crazy, I would never do anything like that." And I'm sure you probably wouldn't. But even if you don't physically harm yourself or your property, anytime you tilt, you're metaphorically stabbing yourself, costing yourself income and self-respect.

As you'll soon see, these wild stories of tilt are only the tip of the iceberg. The more subtle forms of tilt can be just as dangerous, even if they're not as obviously over-the-top.

If you think you don't tilt, all I ask is that you keep an open mind as you read this chapter, and over the next few weeks, as you truly examine your life and your game. I've yet to meet a player who didn't tilt, when they used my definition to examine it.

Any time you deviate from your best strategic decision based on emotion, good or bad, you're tilting.

When you hear that definition, what's your first reaction? Hopefully, it opens your eyes to the full extent of tilt, and how it's not just about smashing computers or rage-tilting away your entire bankroll. Hopefully you can start to see areas of your game where you might be choosing to make emotional decisions instead of strategic ones. When I give this definition, many are surprised about the good emotion part, but it doesn't matter whether the emotion is positive or negative, if it causes you to deviate from A-Game Poker, then it's tilt.

This is why I prefer the term Emotional Decision Making over Tilt. The word tilt has a lot of baggage with it, and many people overlook their tilt because of the images they associate with it. Since it's already such an ingrained part of the poker vernacular, I still use it, but understand that when I say emotional decision-making and tilt, I mean the same thing.

It doesn't matter if the deviation comes from being mad about being 3-bet five hands in a row, or from being overconfident after winning a huge pot, what matters is the choice you make between an emotional decision and your best strategic decision. To illustrate this point further, here are a few examples:

Let's say you're playing an MTT and the action folds to you, having 12 big blinds on the button. And let's say your best strategic decision is to follow a Nash chart, shoving anything that's positive and folding anything that's negative. Remember, I'm not a technical poker coach so I'm not saying this is right or wrong strategically, this is just an example. So, your best strategic decision is to follow this exactly, and you look down at K9 offsuit, which is +0.46, which is a shove. If you say, well, I really don't want to bust right now, I'll wait for something better and fold, that's tilt.

You had an emotion, fear of busting, and deviated from your best strategic decision, which would have been to shove. That's tilt. Now, is it as bad as open-shoving every hand for an hour straight, no, certainly not. But remember, you're making hundreds or thousands of decisions each session, and if those decisions are impacted by tilt, even in a small way, it adds up quickly.

Let's say you're playing a cash game and haven't been able to open a hand in what feels like hours. The Big Blind is a live one and you're desperate to play a pot with them. You look down at King-Six of spades, and it's the prettiest hand you've seen in a while. However, based on the opening range you know is optimal, this should be a fold. You toss in a raise and hope for the best. This is also tilt. Your best strategic decision was to follow your opening ranges, and you had an emotion, in this case you could call it impatience, and you chose to act on that rather than following what you believed to be the best strategic action.

As you can see, the impact of this definition can be game changing. When you look at your game through this lens, it's easy to see situations where your emotions are holding you back from A-Game Poker. As you've read previously in this book, A-Game Players view each hand as an independent puzzle. There shouldn't be an emotion that's changing the way you're solving that puzzle.

Let's say you're in an MTT. You were chip leader, and you've just lost half of your stack. The fact that you were chip leader is completely irrelevant to the next hand. On the next hand, you have a new number of big blinds, you have information on the table, you have an idea of how the different players are playing, how someone may be responding to the fact that they've just doubled up through you, or whatever is happening there, and you just have all of this new information to use to solve a completely new and independent puzzle, which is the puzzle you now have in front of you. If you have the mindset of

"But I was chip leader!"

"I desperately need to get those chips back as quickly as possible."

"That's the person who took those chips from me; I need revenge against them! I'm going to play more pots against them because they're my chips."

Anything along those lines is taking it away from being a puzzle that you're solving and turning it into something personal, something emotional, something that is some version of tilt. Just question yourself as you're playing through:

"Was I solving this in an analytical way?"

That includes, as I said, the emotions of your opponents. Being aware of those emotions is still just analytical and technical information. You also want to factor in how you think your opponents are thinking about you and your emotional state. That's also technical information.

What we don't want are any of these emotions–impatience because you've just lost, anger, anxiety, or anything else—creating these problems for you.

"Each hand, I'm solving a new puzzle. Next hand, I'm solving a new puzzle. I'm always solving a new puzzle."

View the whole game that way, whether you're playing live, cash, online, MTT's. Whatever happened before doesn't matter, except in how it's affected our opponent's mental state; each hand is independent. That's the way that A-Game poker should be played.

Tilt happens in three steps:

1. Trigger
2. Emotion
3. Action

Or T.E.A.

First you have a trigger. This could literally be anything, and what triggers you might not trigger someone else. It could be an outcome at the table, something someone says to you, an internal thought, anything really.

Then you have the emotion, which is also different for each person. Something that triggers anger in one person could trigger amusement in another.

And, finally, you have action. Once you feel an emotion, and take action on it, that's tilt. You could be triggered, feel an emotion, and not act on it, and that wouldn't be tilt.

Now, most of the time when very strong emotions are involved, tilt exists as well. It's important that you don't delude yourself into thinking you can have a powerful emotional reaction, and *not* act on it, unless you're sure this is true.

Let's quickly go back to that last example I gave to show you how this framework works.

Say, you're chip leader of an MTT and you lose half your stack, putting you back to average chips. The outcome of losing the chip lead is the trigger. Next comes the emotion (remember everyone is different here). Maybe you feel sad, maybe you feel angry, maybe you feel frustrated, or maybe you feel nothing at all. Let's use *frustrated* here.

You feel frustrated, and to stop feeling frustrated you try to get back the chips you just lost. The action you take is to widen your ranges and start to gamble more. Those are your chips, and you want them back now. Does that sound familiar? There's a trigger, which leads to an emotion, which leads to an action, which is tilt. Here's a list of common tilt triggers that I've seen in my clients and students.

Playing Outside of Normal Stakes

If you're playing outside of your normal stakes, and your bankroll can't really handle it, that can be a trigger that quite often leads to tilt. It can lead to emotions such as fear, uncertainty, and anxiety.

Facing Continued Aggression

This is incredibly common in the poker world, a lot of players can't cope with continued aggression, like being 3-bet constantly by the same player. It brings up emotions of being picked on or attacked in school and is one of the most common tilt triggers I've seen.

Playing Versus a Weak Player

As funny as it sounds, some people can't cope with people playing bad poker. I get a lot of people coming to me complaining that "I just can't cope with seeing bad plays, plays that don't make sense to me."This is amplified when those plays are rewarded, and even more so if you're the one on the losing end. This can trigger all sorts of emotions such as injustice, greed, impatience, frustration and so on. A situation that should be a dream, quickly turns into a nightmare when tilt leads you to play badly against a very weak opponent.

Prolonged Downswings

When players go through multiple losing sessions in a row, or are getting results much worse than expected, tilt is easily triggered. In fact, what starts off as bad luck often spirals out of control when tilt leads to bad play.

I had a client a few years back who brought up an interesting point. Often when you're going through a downswing it's because you're running into the top of your opponents' ranges more often than you should. He discovered that when this happened it would actually change the range that he gave his opponents, giving them more strong hands than he should. So, while there was no outside appearance of tilt, this subtle change had a dramatic effect on his calculations and led to a significant drop in win rate.

Tilt isn't just a one hand thing; it can literally affect the entire way you think about the game.

Other Examples:

Winning and losing huge pots

Making mistakes

This is obviously a big one, maybe the most dangerous one when it comes to A-Game Players. When you have high expectations for yourself, making a mistake can be a strong trigger.

Others include:

Losing hands they should have won (the bad beat situation)

Losing multiple pots in a row

Going deep in a huge tournament

Getting on a feature table

That can be a huge tilt trigger for people who haven't been on TV before or aren't used to having high levels of attention. I've had players in the past come to me, saying that they could feel themselves self-sabotaging before they got to the final table of a tournament because they knew the final table would be televised, and they didn't feel comfortable playing poker on TV. Obviously, it will destroy your return on investment if you're going to sabotage yourself prior to reaching those television tables.

Once again, have a look at these triggers, or think up some on your own. There is literally an infinite list, and it's all about figuring which ones hit home for you. It's important to categorize the emotions of tilt because that often corresponds with the action that you take.

If you're afraid, often you'll take more timid actions. If you feel overconfident, you'll likely take more loose actions.

Here's a list of common emotions.

Anger

Frustration

Fear

Anxiety

Excitement

Imperviousness - If you feel bulletproof, you'll take big risks that you shouldn't because you feel nothing can go wrong.

Excessively Confident - Confidence is good, but excessive confidence can be incredibly dangerous, and you can find your way into games that you shouldn't be playing in, or making plays that are overly optimistic.

Shame

Grief

Injustice

Ambition

Envy

Ecstasy

Excessive joy when winning - Again, anything too far outside of the normal can be a problem.

Desire

Hopelessness

Once again, it's important to take a look at your triggers and consider which emotions they lead to. When you look at the trigger and emotion together, you can really get a good sense of where this issue is coming from in the first place.

Start to build that in your mind. Start to really create a picture of what's happening here in these moments, why you're feeling this way, and then start to look at your life. What would have made you feel this way? Do you get this same way in other parts of your life?

So, now that we know *how* tilt happens, it's time to examine *why*.

The first reason is simply expectations. When we expect something to happen and it doesn't, it will often trigger an emotional reaction. If you expect your aces to win every time you get them, you'll often react poorly when they don't. This is why getting big hands cracked is such an issue for less experienced players, but doesn't faze those with experience, at least not to the same extent. Now, if you expect not to make big mistakes, then when you do make one, it can cause major issues. If you expect to consistently win, then a prolonged downswing can trigger emotions. If you're playing against a weak player, and expect to win, then losing will be a trigger. I could go on and on about this, but you get the point.

Everyone brings their own issues to the table and has a set of life experiences that are at the heart of who they are and govern their emotional triggers. Given that poker is a game of intense competition, with significant sums of money on the line, these issues can reveal themselves quite quickly and forcefully during the course of a game.

Logically, someone three-betting you four times in a row shouldn't have any emotional impact on you. However, if you were bullied as a child, it can bring back the memory and all the emotions that go along with it. When a trigger in poker is linked to a subconscious program, that program runs, and we experience the emotion that goes along with it. A large part of managing your emotions comes down to managing your expectations.

When you combine an expectation with a negative subconscious program, the emotion involved is amplified significantly. This is something we'll get into in more detail in the section on Detrimental Mental Programs.

This is both an incredibly scary and beautiful aspect of poker. It can reveal serious issues that we have, which are never easy to face. But if we are to master the game, and ourselves, and truly become A-Game Players then we must be willing to look inward.

Why is it that it's particularly difficult for you to have your Aces cracked, even though you got your money in good? Or why is it particularly difficult for you, personally, if you make a mistake? What does making a mistake mean to you as an individual? What does it say about you? Who, in your life, have you worried about revealing your mistakes to? Was it difficult to show your mom and dad your school report if things weren't perfect?

Really start to explore what's going on in your subconscious because oftentimes that's where we'll find very obvious and direct links to the emotional issues that you're having at the poker table.

This is the key takeaway with all of this: That self-exploration is where you'll start to find the freedom from tilt itself, rather than just a Band-Aid.

Now, a brief aside. Through all of this you might be wondering, why would I ever *choose* the emotional decision over the logical one? For some decisions there are physiological reasons that hurt decision making, such as low-energy or high-stress. With Emotional Decision Making, there is a choice being made, sometimes even a very conscious choice to choose the emotional path over the logical one. Have you ever been confident that folding was the right play, but called anyway just to see what they had? You knew better, but still went with emotion. This seems crazy, but it actually makes a lot of sense when you go back to the reason our subconscious exists in the first place.

The truth is that logical, conscious thinking is very hard and takes a lot of energy. Our emotions are designed to ease the burden of our logical mind, by processing lots of data and making a decision for us. This is great from an evolutionary standpoint but can often get us into trouble in the modern world. So, the simple answer as to why we choose emotion over logic is because it's the easiest thing to do. Thinking is hard, which is why most of the world doesn't do too much of it. But A-Game Players aren't most of the world, and rather than let our emotions do the driving, we simply use them as a data point while we keep our hands on the wheel.

So, now that we have an understanding of *how* tilt starts, and *why* it happens, let's talk about *what* we can do about it. Here, we are going to discuss both the bandage *and* the cure. First, we're going to look at how, in the moment, if our emotion has already been triggered, we can stop the negative action from happening. The trigger has gone off, you feel the emotion, and we need to manage that emotion in order to prevent Emotional Decision Making.

Now, this won't necessarily cure tilt, because we have the trigger and the emotion, and once the emotion is there it's not easy to stop. However, if we can step in and soften the blow, we can reduce the damage that you're going to cause to yourself and your bankroll at the table.

There are two reasons why the bandage is important. First, it can be incredibly difficult to eliminate tilt, especially if you're just working on it alone. Second, before you can work on something, you need to know it exists. Sometimes you'll find a trigger you didn't expect and need to deal with it in the moment.

Think of it like a physical injury. You've been in a car crash, and the bandage stops you from dying of blood loss. The stitches, the physical therapy, all of these things, hopefully, will lead to a cure in the end, but meanwhile we've got to put a bandage on it to try to stop death. That's how I want you to look at these strategies. They're not going to solve tilt in its entirety for you, but if they reduce the amount of blood loss, then we'll take it.

The first step to manage tilt in the moment is to notice and name what's actually happening. Be aware of your emotion.

"I'm feeling frustrated."

Call it what it is. Start to see it as something that's passing you by, something that's separate from you.

"I'm feeling anxious."

Ask yourself why you're feeling anxious. Try to create a level of distance between the emotion you're feeling and yourself as a person. Try to separate it subconsciously, so that you're not saying, "I'm angry," but rather saying, "I'm feeling anger; I'm feeling frustration; I'm feeling envy"—or whatever the emotion you're feeling might be.

Anything you can do to start to reduce the emotion to merely a thought in your mind rather than something that's defining you in that moment. As you create that distance between yourself and the emotion, you'll be able to take more control over that emotion.

You've now named that. You're aware that it is present, but that it is separate from you. If you're able to do this, you should be able to maintain your decision-making abilities.

This is another reason I highly recommend a regular meditation habit. This is one of the main skills that you learn when meditating: how to be aware of your emotions and understand that they are more like waves in the ocean than the water itself. Before you can name, you must notice, and meditation will give you the tools to notice the emotion before it's too late.

Again, this doesn't necessarily cure the trigger. The emotion still comes up. You still notice it. It's still there. But when you give yourself distance, you have a much better chance of choosing logic over emotion.

The next step is to take control of your emotions. Once you notice it's there, and understand what you're feeling, you can use visualization to attempt to modulate the emotion. What I like to do here is called:

"The Control Room Visualization"

This is where you picture your mind as a control room, and in that control room you see a console with a dial that has a label that matches the emotion you're feeling. That dial has the numbers 1 through 10 on it, which represent the current level you're feeling of that emotion. Once you know that number you can visualize yourself turning down the dial, lowering the number to whatever you want it to be at.

It goes something like this:

Let's say you're feeling angry. First, close your eyes and ask yourself:

"Where am I from one to ten on anger?"

Put a number on it. You're at a 10.

"Ten, it's a terribly frustrating situation."

Now take a deep breath, and then imagine, in your mind, visualize taking that number down to a nine or an eight, and then decide what that feels like. Again, take another deep breath. Bring that number down to a five or a six. What does that feel like? Accept that any emotion you're feeling in your mind or in your body, because there are physical symptoms, is being created by you. Nothing external can create the emotion. Your mind is creating it, and through visualization, you can start to take control of that.

You can turn that number down. It might not disappear completely, but you can start to take a level of control of it, rather than just running with the emotion, and then having the excuse of *"I was on tilt. It's not my fault."*

I highly recommend trying that at the table the next time your emotions run too high. See how quickly you can learn to reduce that emotional impact when you use these types of visualizations.

The final "In the Moment" tactic is reframing. Again, it's a bandage technique.

This is where you take the current situation, and look at it from another, less emotionally charged angle. You can even use some metaphor and visualization to help penetrate the subconscious, and have it stick more effectively.

For example, I like to use the metaphor of "You are the Casino." Let's say someone just got lucky and put a brutal beat on you. Rather than thinking about how unlucky you are, start to see yourself as a casino running a roulette wheel. Someone hit their number, that's absolutely fine. It's a long-term game. If you start to see this as you running a casino with a house edge, that you're printing money overall, but will consistently see bad beats, you'll consistently see gamblers hitting their number.

That's how your business works. If someone puts a big bet on double zero, and happens to hit it, the casino staff cheers for them, and if their lucky they might even get a room comp or a buffet ticket. It would be absolutely ludicrous for the staff to berate the player saying something like:

"You idiot, how could you ever put so much money on double zero. Don't you know how bad a bet that is? Look at this guy, I bet he can't even spell roulette."

No, that wouldn't happen. And they certainly wouldn't get pissed off and close down the table to prevent you from putting down more action. No, they'd just smile and say, *"Well done, buddy,"* knowing that in the end the money is theirs anyway.

What we are trying to do is reframe the situation and see the world the way it actually is. This is certainly easier said than done in the moment, which is why using metaphor to deliver the logic tends to work better. If you know you have a certain trigger, you can even prepare this ahead of time, so that you can break down your reframe into a simple mantra. Something like:

"I am the casino. I am the casino."

Another reframe I like to use is viewing your entire poker career as a single season of a professional sport. This can be any team sport that you prefer, whether it be soccer, football, baseball or hockey. Most players currently view each session as a complete match. At the end of the session, they see it as having either lost or won the match, depending on if they're up or down. Since we logically know that poker is a long-term game, that's not the correct way to view it. Instead of each session being a match, see each session simply as a single possession. Everyone who plays or watches team sports knows that both teams are going to get the ball, and both teams are usually going to score points.

Basketball is one of the best metaphors for this, as each team is going to score somewhere between 40 and 60 times in a game, and there's a lot of back and forth. Imagine if an NBA player threw a fit every time the other team scored. I don't think they would make it for very long if they had that mindset.

Viewing each session as "just getting the ball," looking at a year as a single match, and your entire career as a season, will reinforce that it's a long-term game, making the short-term swings more manageable.

It's just a lot harder trying to work on the issue when the emotion is alive inside you. It's much more effective to detach the emotion from the trigger, which is what we'll talk about next.

When it comes to curing tilt, things start to get complicated. To fully eliminate any form of tilt you need to step in and disconnect the emotional reaction from the trigger.

If you're going to continue being a poker player, you can't get rid of the trigger, but if your emotional reactions are as severe as the guy who stabbed himself in the leg, then you should probably take a break from poker, at least until you can get yourself sorted.

Learning more about the game and setting better expectations can go a long way in eliminating a good portion of tilt. Maybe losing with aces set you off when you first started, but as you learned how the game works and got more experience, that likely went away. That means that following all the other A-Game recommendations, becoming a student of the game, and properly caring for your mind and body can go a long way in improving decision-making.

However, when it comes to some of the more deep-rooted issues that have formed your Detrimental Mental Programming, that's where things get tricky. This is where I always suggest that you consider working with an expert who has experience in this area. That doesn't necessarily mean working with me. In fact, based on my prices, it really only makes sense for those playing quite high stakes to work with me.

That's why I've trained a team of coaches on the principles of A-Game Poker and on my specific methodology of Mindset & Performance coaching. We have coaches available at investment levels that make sense for all players looking to approach the game in a serious way. When you're looking at your current-day triggers and trying to connect them to events in your past it's almost always more effective and faster to work with someone who specializes in that area.

So, while I can give you some exercises to try on your own, please keep that in mind. And if you're someone playing for a living, at any reasonable stakes, chances are it's going to be a great investment to get those issues resolved sooner rather than later.

The basic principle for resolving tilt, works something like this:

You go find your trigger in poker, or whatever other area of life you're working on, and you observe the emotion that it stirs up inside you. Then you work your way backwards to the first time this emotion came up, which we call the root cause of the issue. Once we know the root cause we can attempt to reframe the emotional connection to the event in order to release or change how you feel about it.

For example, if your trigger is aggression from other players, this might tie back to getting bullied in school. Once we discover that event, we can reframe that situation in a way that empowers you and removes the negative emotion. This might be simply understanding that the actions of a child don't need to affect you as an adult, or by showing empathy to your aggressor and truly understanding, accepting, and forgiving the reasons behind their actions. We go into this in more detail later in the book, and like I said, this is going to be a lot more effective with the help of an experienced performance coach.

A-Game Exercise: Tilt Log

In the resources page for this book, I've included what I call a tilt log.

Make sure to visit: AGamePoker.com/resources to get access to all the extras included with this book

This is a great way to record times when you notice yourself tilting, so you can be prepared when it next happens. This includes a section where you can consider what might be the root cause. You're welcome to give this a try on your own, but don't be discouraged if you're not able to do this part on your own. You may find that the reframes you do on your own are enough. Sometimes just understanding the trigger, will give you enough knowledge to reframe the situation. But if you do end up working with a coach, these logs will go a long way in speeding up the process that they put you through. Ideally, you'll have a tilt log on hand while you play, or at least have some simple notes that you can translate into the log once you're finished with your session.

Here's how the tilt log works:

First, you make note of the situation you found yourself in when you tilted. Second, describe the action you took, how the emotional decision actually manifested. Next, describe the emotion that led to the action. The more specific you can be the better.

Next, estimate the cost of this action. When you do a cost analysis on your tilt, it might be enough to motivate you not to do it in the future. Be honest with yourself here. If you delude yourself into thinking there's no cost, then you'll have no reason to change.

Now describe the trigger. The more specific you can be, the more valuable it is.

The next section asks if you can identify the root cause. Can you think back to another time outside of poker that you felt this way, can you bring it back to the first time you ever felt this way? If so, what was the situation?Remember, you might not be able to determine this on your own, just understand that that's okay.

In the last section, you can reframe the root cause or the specific situation. Obviously, if you don't know the root cause you need to focus on reframing the in-game situation. How can you look at the event or situation differently, in a way that empowers you and reduces the emotion from the trigger? Is it possible there's any benefit to the situation? If so, what would that look like?

Remember, you likely can't eliminate the trigger, but you do get to control how you view it. Choose to view it in a way that allows you to continue playing your A-Game, to continue to make the best decisions you possibly can.

CHAPTER 23

THE RECOVERY PHASE

Recovery is where the A-Game Player dominates the competition. Not only is our short-term performance improved through recovery, but we create legitimate staying power during the process. By embracing each of the three phases of the A-Game Engine, A-Game Players have the speed and power of the hare and the consistency and determination of the tortoise, all in one package.

Poker is a game that requires an expenditure of considerable mental resources to perform at a high level. In essence, recovery is the opposite of performance. To perform you must expend resources, and recovery is the process through which those resources are recouped, so that you have the ability to expend them again when it comes time to perform.

In poker, these resources are typically considered to be mental, but if you've ever played a long session where you perceived the stakes to be high, you'll know that it can be just as physically taxing as it is mentally.

Without sufficient recovery, A-Game Poker is not attainable. The Recovery Phase builds recovery systems into your daily, weekly, monthly, and yearly life.

Have you ever experienced a time when the thought of playing or studying poker made you physically cringe? Where just the thought of firing up your computer and looking at the lobby, or getting in the car and driving to the casino drained you of most of your energy?

Have you ever gone through a period where the only way you would play is if you forced yourself to do so, and even then you had almost no focus and could only play very short sessions?

If any of those ring true for you, then chances are you have experienced burnout. And even if you haven't experienced this in poker, chances are you've had it for something else in your life. Maybe it was a sport you played as a child that you really didn't like but your family forced you to play anyway. Maybe it was a job where you were expected to put in massive amounts of work and had little time off. Or maybe it was in school, studying for a huge exam or working on a major project. It's a problem that most of us have experienced, and a growing problem in the world today.

Burnout is the antithesis of A-Game Poker, and is the result of constantly exposing your mind and body to stress, without giving it a chance to recover. Eventually you get to the point where your body can't take it anymore, and you go into a state of repulsion from the activity causing the stress. It's kind of like the reaction that your body creates if you've ever gotten extremely sick from excess consumption of a particular alcoholic beverage. If the incident is bad enough, you can be repulsed by the mere smell of alcohol or that particular type of alcohol, an effect that can last years, sometimes even for the rest of your life. This is simply your body's way of protecting itself from something harmful. Now, with the alcohol example it's likely a plus EV reminder not to go overboard, but when the thought of playing poker becomes physically repulsive, that's a big problem, especially if it's your primary means of income.

That's why proper recovery is so vital, and why it's the true secret weapon of the A-Game Player. If you don't recover in an intentional way, your body and mind will force you to do so at some point. When that happens, when you enter an involuntary burnout phase, you lose much of your control. It can often take weeks or months to recover from a particularly bad case of burnout, and in many cases it's enough to end a poker career for good.

When people think in terms of recovery and burnout prevention, the first thing that usually comes up is the idea of life balance. Life balance is one of those terms that nearly everyone seems to get wrong, and you end up with extreme arguments on both sides of the question of what it means. One side says the only way to be successful is to hustle and grind 24/7, and if you're not one hundred percent obsessed and engrossed in what you're doing then you might as well not even try. The other side says that the key to life is in finding perfect balance and harmony in every area at all times. If every area of your life isn't given equal weight, then everything will just break and fall apart. Being an A-Game Player, you should be able to see the absurdity of both of these rather didactic arguments.

If you were to try to focus on something for every waking hour of the day, we all know that performance would suffer pretty quickly, and burnout would eventually set in. On the other hand, in order to make big strides in certain areas, we occasionally need to give specific areas of our life a high level of attention, even at the temporary expense of other areas. In order to find the optimal approach, we need to take a more nuanced approach, something that I call Strategic Imbalance.

In my framework, an A-Game Player will always be in one of the three Phases of Preparation, Performance, or Recovery.

In order to achieve optimal results, you do need to find the correct balance between these areas. That does not mean that each day needs to be 100 percent balanced between the three. Just like poker is a long-term game, so is the game of optimal performance.

The key is to take the vision statement that you created for yourself earlier, and figure out what the correct balance is to get you closer to that vision right now, and strategically unbalancing yourself in order to achieve that optimally.

If you visualize the Three Phases as pie charts, this is what a reasonably balanced day would look like:

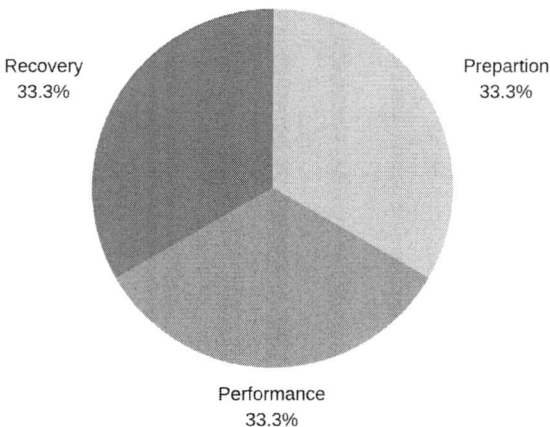

Recovery
33.3%

Prepartion
33.3%

Performance
33.3%

You have equal parts Preparation, Performance, and Recovery. Now, don't make the mistake of trying to correlate percentages of the pie directly with hours, think of it more in terms of energy. An intense 6-hour session, won't take exactly 6 hours of recovery. You'll have 8 hours of sleep plus whatever number of waking hours are necessary to reset and get you ready to Perform again.

Now, as I said, the goal here isn't necessarily to find that perfect balance each day, it's about figuring out what ratio is ideal right now, and balancing everything out over the long term.

Every action you take has consequences, both positive and negative. How you invest your time now has a big impact on the results of your future, and an A-Game Player is adept at weighing the options they have, and choosing the right ones.

As an example let's take someone who is just getting started in the game. For them, their Life Balance Pie Chart, in terms of their poker game, would look something like 50% Recovery 35% Preparation 15% Performance.

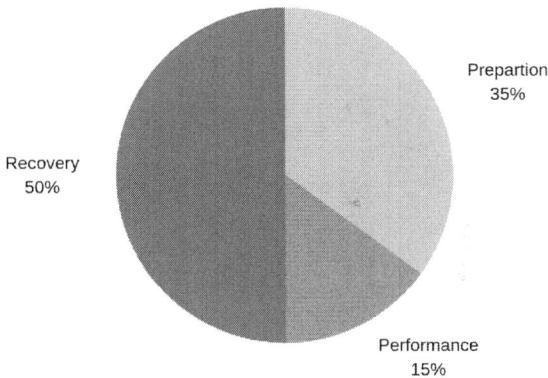

They need to invest time into improving their skills, so the balance goes to Preparation.

Now let's say you're a nosebleed high-stakes pro, and there is a wealthy VIP in town who loves having you in their game. Imagine getting a text saying the game is about to start and you should head to the poker room right away, and you respond:

"Sorry, I'll pass. I need to make sure I get in enough study time today."

That's probably not going to happen, and choosing to prepare rather than Perform in that moment would be a very big mistake. Let's say they're in town for a few weeks. Well, in that scenario the ratios might look something like 50% Recovery, 45% Performance, and 5% Preparation.

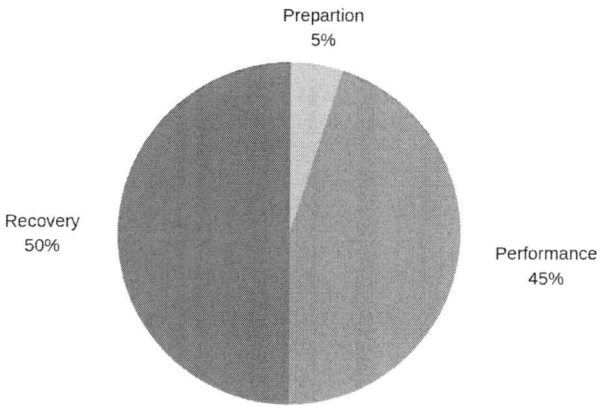

Prepartion
5%

Recovery
50%

Performance
45%

Now, once they leave, the Preparation and Performance percentages might swap, as you have more down time waiting for the next big game to fire off.

Another example that's similar to this would be a big MTT series, either live or online. For an MTT player, that's your time to shine. You'll want to put your focus into Performing and worry about improving your game at a later date. Here, you're either performing or recovering and the ratio might look something like 50% Recovery 49% Performance and 1% Preparation.

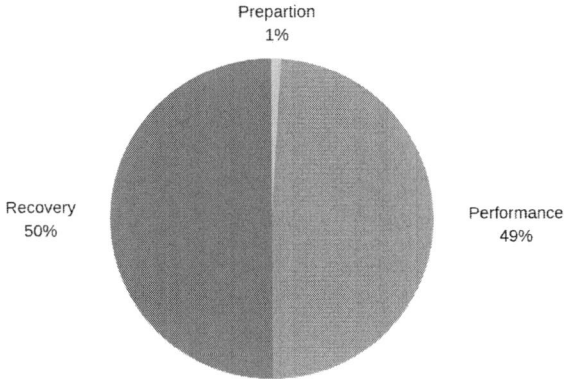

Prepartion
1%

Recovery
50%

Performance
49%

Now, let's say that the tournament series comes to an end, and you weren't able to 100 percent recover each day during the series. Well in that situation you might need to spend a week that is 100 percent recovery, maybe going for a quick holiday or laying low and relaxing for a few days before you jump back into the grind.

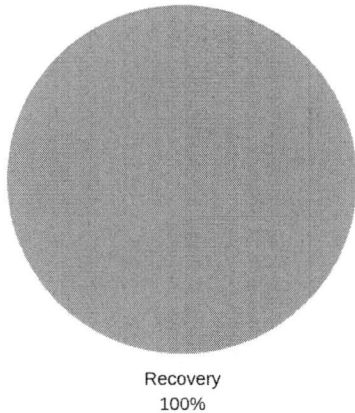

Recovery
100%

Now, you might have noticed something about those pie charts that I just showed. In all of them, no matter what side of balance they were on, all of them still had a significant portion dedicated to recovery. Recovery is something that will always be present, whether you focus on it or not.

If you don't believe me, try going two days straight without sleep and let me know what happens. Actually, please don't do that. That would be a horrible idea, and I just suggested it to make my point clear.

Simply to survive, your body needs to maintain at least a minimum level of recovery. As an A-Game Player, you're not simply looking for the minimum amount of recovery to survive, you're looking for the optimal amount to thrive. Because without sufficient recovery, A-Game Poker is not attainable. The truth is, most people looking to achieve high-performance try to do so while getting by on as little recovery as possible. They think if they cut their sleep short by two hours, that they gain two hours of performance, when in fact they are just gaining more hours of subpar performance. More is not better, better is better.In almost every scenario an hour of A-Game will be a whole lot more valuable than 3 hours of D-Game.

At this point, hopefully you've completely bought into the concept I've outlined and are ready to put it into action. And just in case you're not, let me hammer it home with this: You are not a magical unicorn who can perform optimally with little to no recovery. Now repeat that with me one more time (yes, say it out loud).

"I am not a magical unicorn who can perform optimally with little to no recovery."

I've worked with many of the very best poker players in the world, and I've still yet to find anyone whose performance and profits did not go up by putting an additional focus on optimizing their recovery.

With that cleared up, let's jump into the "How" of the Recovery Phase.

PRO CASE STUDY

KRISTEN FOXEN

THREE-TIME GPI FEMALE PLAYER OF THE YEAR & FOUR-TIME WSOP BRACELET WINNER

I've never had an issue putting in volume, in fact quite the opposite. I would consistently put in 24-36 hour sessions, for no good reason at all. I would tell myself...

"One more hour, one more hour"

...and then finally the sun was rising again and I realized I'd missed another night of sleep as one more hour had turned into eight hours or more.

If I was approaching things rationally, I would have just stopped after 8-10 hours, gone to bed, and started again tomorrow. It's not like there was anything special with the games, I just felt compelled to keep playing until I physically couldn't push myself anymore. I was at the point where I was putting in multiple sessions like this each week and then spending days recovering from the toll they put on my mind and body.

This was when I first reached out to Elliot to start working on my mindset. What drew me into poker in the first place was the ability to live and breathe the game 24/7. If I wasn't physically playing, I could be discussing it with friends or running through spots in my head. I told myself that I got into poker because of the freedom it allowed, but just the thought of taking a day off gave me anxiety. I couldn't go out with friends, relax, or even have fun outside of the game. I would worry about the EV I was missing out on, scared that a once-in-a-lifetime game would happen to form when I was out. I could go to dinner with poker friends, but if the topic shifted away from game talk, that anxiety would pop up, and I felt a pull to steer it back in that direction or leave and go play.

Working with Elliot made me realize that I had created a subconscious program telling me my self-worth was directly connected to how hard I worked. My parents worked long hours, took little time off, and ran a successful and profitable business. Somewhere it was imprinted upon me that my worth came from being successful, and being successful was only possible through hard work and deep sacrifice.

Anyone looking from the outside could tell that how I approached my game was not optimal. Instead of playing 8 hours a day, six days a week, I would play two 24-hour sessions with two recovery days in between. That meant I was fresh and alert less than 25% of the time, rather than the 75%+ I would have been doing it the standard way.

You would think this would be obvious, but what Elliot taught me was that strong subconscious programs have a much stronger pull than common sense. During our sessions, Elliot and I were able to untangle the connection between success, self-worth, and grinding myself to the bone, and that's when my results started to take off.

I started viewing the game of poker as a tool to create my ideal life. I still worked very hard at the game, but I made sure that the times and places I put that energy towards were those where the return would be the greatest. Before, my marker for success was how painful and how much sacrifice I felt to achieve it. Now, I just let the success speak for itself.

Before, if I got results and it felt easy, I had to double down because I believed that success had to feel bad. If something came easy, it meant that you weren't working hard enough. Now, I understand that there are many spots where being smarter has much higher leverage than working harder.

I understand that playing my A-Game in a smaller window is much more profitable than playing my C-Game during a marathon session. Not only have I been able to thrive results-wise with this new outlook and approach, and my life is so much better for it.

I can go to the gym, spend time with friends, focus on my relationship, and take days off, and not only am I able to set poker to the side, I'm able to see how these activities improve my results rather than just being a way to fill time in between sessions.

It's hard to explain how big of a shift this has been. It's like I'm looking at life through a whole different lens, one that's a whole lot more fun and fulfilling. The biggest takeaway is that you can have it all with the right approach. There isn't a dichotomy between happiness and success. Happiness can be one of the most powerful ways to fuel your success.

That doesn't mean things are never hard, you won't have any bumps along the way, or you'll never have to grind through some tough times; those are all a natural part of life. It means that being the best version of yourself is how you unlock your highest levels of performance, something that's not possible when you push yourself in destructive and unsustainable ways. The best part is that I can now enjoy my success and feel proud of my achievements.

Poker is still a massive part of my life, which I control and use as a tool to reach my goals and live my best life.

CHAPTER 24

POST SESSION ROUTINE

Imagine you have a rubber band. You take it between your first fingers and thumbs, and stretch it out as far as it can go without breaking. This state represents the Performance phase. Fully engaged and stretched to the max of your capabilities. Now, you have two options. In the first, you let go of the rubber band, which will return (somewhat violently) to its original state, likely giving your hand a bit of a snap in the process.

This is how most players transition from Performance to Recovery, and more accurately some ill-defined state that is neither Preparation, Performance, nor Recovery. Finishing a session, they immediately transition into the rest of their day without allowing their mind to cool down from the Performance state or get closure on the session. This causes them to hold onto their emotions, ruminating about the outcome, or over hands they were uncertain about. In turn, this carries over into their personal life, preventing them from being present with friends and family. It can even cause sleep issues, as they replay hands from the session over and over again in their minds. So, that's rubber band option one.

The other option is to slowly release the tension, dissipating the energy that was stored up in that stretched circle of rubber. This method allows you to go from the active state to the resting state, smoothly and without anyone getting hurt. This is what we're looking to do with our Post-Session Routine.

A Post-Session Routine is a process for reviewing and analyzing your performance, detaching from the session, and transitioning to the Recovery Phase.

There is a concept called the Zeigarnik Effect, which refers to the mind's tendency to remember uncompleted tasks over completed tasks. This was first observed in waitstaff, who could remember every specific detail of a table's order before the food was served but would lose that memory as soon as their task was completed and the food was delivered to the table. It's also prominently used in television shows through the use of cliffhangers. Nearly every episode in a television serial (i.e. a show with a continuing plot that unfolds in a sequential episode-by-episode fashion), will end with a cliffhanger. If the producers have done a good job and have gotten you to care about what happens next, you'll literally feel compelled to watch the next episode, just to get closure. This is why you can sit down to watch one episode of a new show on Netflix and all of a sudden it's two days later and you're halfway through season 3 of the show.

Another term for this effect is an Open Loop. When you begin a task or a thought but don't complete it, you're said to have opened a loop. Closing the loop is when you've finished the task or taken action on the thoughts. The Zeigarnik Effect is simply your mind prioritizing the open loops vs the closed loops.

As we well know, poker is a game of incomplete information. That means you'll run into many scenarios where you'll make a decision but then won't get the full closure of knowing whether or not it was the right play. Maybe you're playing a massive pot and end up making a huge laydown on the river. Even if you're quite certain that it was the right play, it can often create an open loop that's difficult to close. You can easily run into double digit situations like this throughout a session, and it's easy to see how this can continue to consume your mind even after you've stopped the session.

Now, there are certainly situations where the Zeigarnik Effect can be used positively, such as the example of the waitstaff that serves meals and immediately afterwards sheds the now-useless order information. An open loop might even be useful in a poker context, as you hold on to a situation that is valuable for you to study precisely because it has stayed in your mind. It's a reflection of your uncertainty, which makes it worth examining and solving with an eye to the future.

The problem comes when there is a big gap between when the loop opens and when it closes. Keeping the loop open can prevent you from going into recovery and, as a consequence, it can have a negative impact on your life outside poker. If the rubber band remains fully stretched, it forces you to continue expending energy, which means that situations that are meant to recover energy are actually in the background siphoning it off. If you've ever finished a session and found it difficult to connect and be present with friends and family, then you know the feeling I'm talking about.

With the Post-Session Routine, you get to either close that loop immediately, or set a time to do so in the future, which will close the loop for the time being. From there you can go about your day, and start to get the mental recovery that your mind needs in order to perform at its best the next time you play.

All right, so let's break down what I've found to be the ideal format for a post-session routine.

First there is Review,

Then Analyze,

and finally Detach.

Review

The US Army developed a process called an After Action Review. This is a structured review conducted after an action is taken where the intended results are compared to the achieved results. This serves as a feedback loop where you can take an objective look at the results of an action, and discover areas that can be improved the next time the action is taken.Given that this is a powerful method of improvement, it has quickly spread to the business, sports, and performance worlds.

As part of the Post-Session Routine, a quick review allows you to compare the goals and intentions you started your session with, and see how they actually played out in-game. It allows you to quickly pinpoint some areas you might need to focus on, both in your mental and technical games. Between the Review and Analyze steps, most, if not all of the open loops can be closed, allowing you to Detach and transition into Recovery.

I've found that asking and answering these five simple questions is the best way to perform an effective review of your session in the shortest amount of time possible. Many of my clients find it most useful to actually answer these questions by hand, whether in a physical journal or a digital text document. You can also ask yourself these questions in your head, although that will do more for closing loops than it will for making long-term adjustments. If, for whatever reason, that's your only option at the time, it's still better than snapping the rubber band back too quickly.

If you play multiple sessions in a day you can do the PSR after your last session of the day or go through a condensed version at the end of any early sessions.

Here are the questions you should ask yourself during review:

What happened during the session?

Here is where you give a brief, objective, and drama-free synopsis of your session. Leave out the judgment, and just put in the facts.

Next, ask yourself:

Did you accomplish your pre-session goals? If not, why?

In your A.G.A.M.E. routine you set some pre-session goals. Now is the time to compare your intended results with your actual results. Remember, your pre-session goals aren't going to be monetary, as that isn't something you can control. Your goals are areas of focus or specific spots you need to pay extra attention to, not goals to just win a bunch of money. So, take a look at your intentions and if what actually happened is different than what you intended, try to figure out why.

Now, ask yourself:

What went well?

People tend to focus their reviews only on the negative, but it can be equally beneficial to figure out what went well, so you can reinforce that behavior or action in the future. Did your aces get cracked and you didn't blink an eye? Well, commend yourself for that as that will increase your confidence in your mindset going forward.

The next question is:

What roadblocks did you encounter?

Did a Detrimental Mental Program rear its ugly head? Did you run into a spot where you felt completely lost? Did you lose focus and struggle to get it back? When you start to understand the roadblocks you encounter, especially the ones that seem to pop up over and over again, you'll know what where you need to put in the most work going forward, which leads me to the last question:

What can you do to address those roadblocks in the future?

Here is where you set some intentions for improving areas that you're struggling with. This isn't necessarily about coming up with the fix immediately, although if you can that's great, but more than likely it's going to be something you need to address in a study session or with off-the-table A-Game work. In the moment, creating a plan will do a great job of closing the loop, getting it out of your head and into a plan of action.

Analyze

The next step in the P.S.R. is Analyze. This is where you run through a short study session with the specific goal of closing any open loops.

This could be a 5-minute rundown of the one hand that bugged you, to a quick 30-minute ministudy session going through hands you marked in your database software or took notes on live. Some people even choose to place a full 60-90 minute study session here, if it's where it fits best in your schedule. That's more of a convenience and scheduling thing. For most people it will be on the shorter side, with the specific goal of closing any loops.

Now, during the Analyze phase you don't necessarily have to do a full breakdown of the hands in question. Deferring them to a future study session, or making a plan for when you'll work on that hand or spot, usually does just as good of a job closing the loop as actually working through to an answer. In this way the Analyze step can be an extension of the last review question, where you process hands and plan how you'll work through roadblocks. However you handle this step, just make sure that it scratches any itches you developed during the session, so you're able to fully detach from the session and continue on with your day.

Detach

The final step of the post-session routine is Detach. In Review and Analyze you worked to close any open loops and started to ease yourself out of the Performance Mindset. In Detach, we complete the transition by putting your mind in a relaxed state, so it can begin to Recover.

The first step to detaching is to remove yourself from your work environment, whether that be your online grind station, the poker room, or the tournament hall, in order to get the best detachment you need to switch environments. Now, this isn't 100 percent necessary, it is possible to perform a detachment exercise on your playing computer, or at the casino, but to get the best possible results you'll want to shift environments.

The next step in Detach is to perform some sort of low-attention but enjoyable exercise. The easiest way to do this is with any of my Post-Session Cool-Down audios, one of which is available on the resources page at AGamePoker.com/resources.

These are specifically designed to detach you from the session and begin the recovery process that's necessary to keep you playing your best over the long term. If you're looking for the easiest and most effective way to detach, you'll definitely want to check out the resources I've provided.

That being said, it's not your only option. Anything that is relatively mindless and enjoyable can work well. Meditation can obviously work well here and can be a good substitute if you don't have my audios available. This is also a good opportunity to participate in some of your guilty pleasures, things that might not look like high-performance activities on the surface but give you enjoyment. I'm talking about stuff like video games, YouTube videos, TV shows, building Lego, catching up on social media, group chats, and so on.As long as it's something you enjoy that isn't poker related and doesn't induce stress, it's probably a fine fit here.

The point is simply to detach from the game and give your mind some space to start to recover. This will usually be relatively short, something like 10 to 20 minutes, and putting it directly at the end of your session means you can transition into the rest of your life and leave the game behind for a while.

You might have some other longer leisure activities planned for the rest of the day, but we want to detach immediately at the end of a session, so you don't end up carrying your session with you. So, let's say you plan to go to the gym after your last session of the day. I wouldn't classify that as a detachment exercise, as it can take you some time to get ready and get there. If you had a home gym and could go almost immediately from Analyze to exercising, then I would consider it detachment. Otherwise, no.

Anyway, there you have it, the PSR or Post-Session Routine. You now have a simple but effective system for disconnecting from your session, allowing you to transition into the Recovery Phase. Interestingly, because it comes at the end of the session when your work is "done," a lot of players tend to leave this phase out. But not A-Game Players. An A-Game Player understands that the post-session routines are just as important as the pre, if they want to maintain performance over the long run.

A-Game Exercise: Implement P.S.R.

With the post-session review, you now have a third system to implement in the performance phase. Just like I asked you not to implement the A-Game Audit at the same time as the pre-session protocol, I want you to hold off on implementing the P.S.R. until after you've completed both of those exercises.

Once you've done that I'd like you to dedicate yourself to doing three post-session reviews in your notebook or document, and then once you've completed all three, spend some time analyzing the differences you notice by adding this system into your game.

Pro Case Study

BenCB

High-Stakes MTT Professional & Founder of Raise Your Edge

Success is simple, but not easy.

To be a great poker player, you must study the game, play a lot of hands, review your game, make adjustments, and repeat that cycle as many times as possible. To run a great business, you need to solve a big enough problem, and then let those with the problem know you exist. Mix that with some luck, and you'll be good to go.

The problem is consistently taking the actions you know you should be doing. That's where Elliot comes in. In my Twitch Streams, the comment I get most often is...

"How do you stay so calm during these brutal sessions?"

I owe much of that to the work I've done with Elliot. However, the most significant shift since I began working with him is my ability to quiet my mind and disconnect when needed.

Between poker and my two businesses, I was on the computer grinding away all day, and when I would finally step away, I'd finally have time to think, and my mind would flood with thoughts and ideas.

Before working with Elliot, I struggled with quieting that voice, leading to poor sleep and an inability to disconnect and recover fully. In poker and business, you need to keep your mind sharp, which means strategically disconnecting and giving your batteries time to recharge.

That doesn't mean you have an excuse to play video games or scroll social media all day. It means knowing when you're at the point where your capacity to do good work is diminished and shifting gears to recovery mode.

I'll always be a grinder, but no longer grind myself down. After working with Elliot, I can disconnect, quiet my mind, recharge, and return stronger than ever. Working hard will make you great. Working hard and strategically recovering will make you elite.

CHAPTER 25

SYSTEMS FOR SLEEP

Quality sleep and poker are topics that seem to be as far apart as you can get.

The most profitable poker is played when the majority of people in the surrounding community are fast asleep. Or, put another way, poker players are in the Performance Phase when the rest of the world is in Recovery. Weekends and evenings are when the recreational money comes to play, and that's where you'll find an A-Game Player. This leads to many professional poker players living a night-shift lifestyle, where they sleep during the day and are up late at night.

The irregular hours of the game can easily lead to disrupted sleep patterns. A tournament player might bust early or run deep into the night. A cash game player might find themselves in a game that feels too profitable to leave. There are even some large private games where the professionals are expected to put in 48 hours straight with very few breaks.

Serious recreational players don't have it any easier. An A-Game-minded amateur is essentially working two jobs, their conventional job during the day and poker in the evening and on weekends.

There's no doubt that keeping a consistent sleep schedule as a poker player is challenging. Yes, there are some time zones where online players can manage something similar to a conventional job's schedule; we even discussed that as a large advantage earlier in the book.

In addition to the ways poker is antithetical to quality sleep, there is also a tendency that high-performers have to expand their working hours and neglect sleep with the idea that it will allow them to be more productive. In taking this approach, high-performance-minded poker players will quickly find themselves on the path to burnout, a trap that A-Game Players know to avoid at all costs. The fact that it is difficult to discipline oneself in this way means there is a large advantage to be had by optimizing an area that others completely neglect.

In my experience, optimizing your sleep is one of the most +EV systems you can implement into your life. A few weeks of shifting from a state of even subtle sleep deprivation to one of high-quality sleep has been described to me by many of my clients like a fog lifting from their life. Here's the thing:

Only a very small percent of the population are what's called short sleepers; i.e. the rare individual who can function at a high level with little sleep. Yet, if you asked the poker playing community, almost everyone thinks that they are in that very small minority.

That's the problem with sleep deprivation. It impairs your brain function at such a level that when you are deprived, you're likely unaware of it. it. So, if you're not getting proper sleep now, the chances are you're underperforming without realizing it.

If you do fall into the category of chronically sleep deprived, and this is the only system you implement in this entire book, I'll wager you'll still feel like the cost of the investment has been worthwhile. And not just in performance at the table, but in overall health and quality of life.

Before we go into solutions, let's look at some of the negatives of sleep deprivation. A group of researchers from the University of New South Wales, in Australia, conducted a study comparing sleep deprivation with alcohol consumption. They found that someone who was awake for 19 hours straight and took a concentration test, performed on a par with someone who had a blood alcohol count of point-zero-five percent (which is legally drunk in Australia), and someone who was awake for 28 straight hours performed as if they had a blood alcohol count of point one percent. Now, imagine you're playing a marathon session while having a few drinks, and you'll see that your performance goes right down the drain. And it's not just extreme sleep deprivation that's the problem.

At the University of Wisconsin, a performance test was run on subjects who had been deprived just one hour per night over a 10-day period against those who had pulled an all-nighter. Surprisingly, they performed at similar levels.

If you struggle with fitness and nutrition, it might actually be lack of sleep that's the root cause. A study published in the European Journal of Clinical Medicine showed when you're sleep deprived it causes a hormone imbalance which throws off your sense of hunger, causing you to eat up to 300 extra calories per day.

Studies have also shown a reduction in memory, creativity, and emotional control when sleep deprived. So many of the common mental game problems I run into can largely be resolved by getting proper sleep.

It's such a common mindset in today's world to wear lack of sleep as a badge of honor. It feels like cutting off an hour or two of sleep means you can get so much more done each day. The truth is, all it really means is you perform worse over a longer period of time. This is not something you can afford to do, both for your long-term health and your win rate. My friend, Dr. Michael Breus, likes to say:

"Sleep is a High-Performance Event."

It's a great mindset to have.

My A-Game Poker Masterclass includes a bonus seminar with Dr. Michael Breus called: Sleep For High-Performance Poker. Visit: AGamePoker.com/resources to claim your discount on the course.

Most of us simply think of sleep as a necessary evil rather than embracing the edge it can give us. I'm going to show you some key factors and systems to get the most out of your sleep, and I'm confident this is a spot where many of you will push back and tell me why it won't work for you.

Yes, there are certain situations where there are very good games at odd hours, and many locations where the best games run deep into the night.

In those cases you need to realize two things:

1) That you're giving up a lot of performance by maintaining that type of schedule, so make sure to factor that into your decision.

and 2) that if you choose to stick with awkward sleep hours, you should still implement as much of this stuff as possible.

Even if you don't get it perfect, you'll still be better off doing some of it than none of it. The truth is, most poker players would be better off creating their playing schedule around their sleeping schedule rather than the other way around. I've had many online

MTT clients see a massive boost in success once they moved from Europe to North or Central America. The schedule just makes it so much easier to maintain a normal sleep cycle and reap the performance rewards that go along with good sleep.

While it's easy to talk about morning routines, you don't hear as much about sleep routines. The truth is, if I could only choose one or the other for my clients I would pick a sleep routine every time. Remember, sleep is a high-performance event, and it should be treated with the same respect you'd have before sitting down to play in a big game.

The general guideline for sleep is eight hours in bed. This is a bit misleading because most people think of that as eight hours of sleep. The data shows that the actual number is around 7.5 hours of sleep for most people. Each sleep cycle is around one and a half hours long, and most people need around five sleep cycles, which comes out to be 7.5 hours of sleeping time. It takes the average person around 20 minutes to fall asleep, which takes you to right around the eight hours in bed that most people talk about.

Our Circadian rhythm influences our sleep and wake cycles, and controls all sorts of bodily functions such as hormone release, body temperature, eating, and digestion. While your Circadian Rhythm can adjust with time, having inconsistent sleep times really throws things off. If you've ever had jet lag, you'll know exactly what this feels like. That's why having a consistent wake-up time is so important for long-term health.

This means the ideal scenario would be waking up at just about the same time everyday, seven days a week. So, the first part of creating your Sleep System is to choose your wake-up time. As light and dark cycles have a big impact, the ideal wake time is sometime between 6 and 8 am, but many poker players will likely push it a bit later. Once you have your wake time, you can just subtract 7.5 hours and then you have your falling asleep time. Congrats, that's the first step for your sleep system!

With your bedtime lined up, you'll want to build a Nighttime Routine that prepares you to get the best sleep possible. But first let's talk about your surroundings.

Environment

To set yourself up for sleep success you'll need a proper environment.

Your bed and mattress is priority #1 when it comes to your sleep environment. Spending every night sleeping on a crappy mattress is the equivalent of playing nosebleed cash games from a 15-year-old laptop that's full of malware. Sure it's technically possible, but you're losing a ton of EV taking that approach. Take time to find a proper mattress that is comfortable and supportive. It's non negotiable. You're going to be spending at least 8 hours a day on this piece of furniture, so you might as well invest in the best you can afford. Do your research and buy accordingly.

Another important factor is light. The ideal sleep situation is pitch black. If you're trying to set up the ideal sleep environment for the first time you'll be amazed at just how many of your electronics have annoying little LED lights that are always on. Either unplug those or purchase coverups stickers that are sold in lots of places. Investing in some high quality blackout blinds is also important, especially if you're going to be sleeping at any point when the sun is out, or if you live in a city with lots of street lights.

The third key factor is temperature. Temperature plays into your circadian rhythm, which means you'll want a nice cool room in order to get your best ever sleep.

Other factors to consider are caffeine use and alcohol consumption. You should aim to have your last caffeinated beverage eight hours before bedtime and avoid consuming alcohol for at least three hours before you go to bed. If you drink, you should also have one glass of water for every drink you consume, to mitigate the negative effects on sleep. There will certainly be times when you need to strategically use caffeine to stay alert in an exceptional game, but try to make it the exception rather than the rule.

You should give as much thought to this as you would to a morning routine or a pre-session warm up. You can test out many different things, but here are a few suggestions for things I've found to work well.

First, give yourself an hour to wind down. Ideally, you turn off all electronic devices, as the blue light they emit can damage your circadian rhythm. If you want to go all in, you can try out some blue blocker glasses to shield you from that spectrum completely. Many of my clients have had great results doing both. This can be a great time to meditate or do other stress relief and breathing exercises. Journalling is a very popular addition to a nighttime routine, and if you're someone who often holds onto their thoughts, this is a great way to get them out of your head so you can fall asleep quickly. Reading fiction can be another great way to set your mind up for an easy transition. I would generally avoid non-fiction and poker content, as those activate your mind more than they help cool it down.

The typical player views sleep as a barrier to poker performance, while an A-Game Player understands that it is a tool they can use to gain a considerable edge over their opponents. In a land of sleep-deprived poker players, the well rested player is king.

A-Game Exercise: Create Your Sleep Routine

Alright, time to get out that notebook or document again. This time, it will be deciding how much time you want to dedicate to this routine, and which of the suggestions you'll start to implement immediately. Remember, this isn't about getting everything perfect all at once. The systems you create today will not be the same a year from now and beyond. You'll implement, review, adjust and iterate them, just as you do with any other part of your game.

Sleep is essential, but do not beat yourself up if you're not able to create a sleep system that is as consistent and dialed in as someone working a conventional job. Rather than trying to fit a square peg into a round hole, the job of an A-Game Player is working with the circumstances in front of them, and optimizing from there.

CHAPTER 26

RECOVERY STRATEGIES

My favorite framework for recovery comes from a paper called "The Recovery Experience Questionnaire" published in the Journal of Occupational Health Psychology, where researchers Sabine Sonnentag and Charlotte Fritz proposed four strategies for recovery, which they called Recovery Experiences. They are:

- Psychological Detachment
- Relaxation
- Mastery
- Control

From my own experience there is another category that I've found to be particularly powerful, which I call Anti-Focus.

I'll run through each of these recovery strategies, so you can start to build your own arsenal of recovery tools that fit best in your life. On that note, something that's important to remember is that recovery is different for everyone, and the key is to find what works best for you.

For some people massages are incredibly relaxing, and for others they are incredibly uncomfortable and can actually cause stress and anxiety. The key is to focus on each of the recovery categories as principles, and fill in the activities that work best for you.

Detachment

When I talk about detachment I'm talking about both physically and mentally detaching from the game. It's one thing to get up from the game, it's another to remove the game from your mind.

Previously, we talked a good bit about detachment, and you'll be using your PSR as the first step in mentally detaching from the game during recovery. It's typical to find poker players who really struggle with this aspect. It can even get to the point where they have trouble interacting with non-poker players or participating in activities that don't involve poker. In their mind, recovery is browsing through the forums and participating in group chats, and maybe even going out to dinner with some poker friends who end up talking poker the whole time.

Now, there's a certain level of dedication to the game–some would say even obsession–that is common amongst the best players in the world. It's a level of thought and attention to the game that may well be necessary to get to the top, but when it gets to the point of where it's totally consuming to the exclusion of everything else, it becomes a problem. Especially when considering desired longevity in the game.

I've worked with a lot of players who struggle with this issue, and all of them have seen benefits by balancing their obsession with detachment, both in the short term and in the long term. So, really take a look at your life and see how much time you spend completely detached from the game. If you're like most serious poker players, it's probably a lot less than you think.

Relaxation

A relaxation activity is something that requires little energy and is enjoyable.

There are a wide range of activities that fall into this category, so it's worth exploring a variety of them to find what works best for you. Meditation, yoga, massage,visualization exercises (such as those found in my Primed Mind app) are all activities that are generally considered relaxing.

Saunas and steam rooms are great options, as there is some promising research showing they have immense health benefits in the long term, in addition to improving mood and mental focus. One study showed that men who used the sauna four to seven times per week had a 40% reduction in all-cause mortality, compared to those who only used it once per week. That's a seriously nice side effect for something that many find incredibly relaxing. Any time you can get other positive side effects from your recovery activities, it's a nice bonus.

Something as simple as going for a walk or hike, especially in a more natural setting, is one of the best relaxation activities out there. Video games, movies, board game night, comedy shows, concerts, and dancing are other activities in this category. The list is nearly endless. All that matters is that the activity doesn't require much energy expenditure and that you find it enjoyable.

Chances are you have a few ideas about relaxation activities already. Maybe you even feel guilty for doing them, and beat yourself up for slacking off when you could be studying or playing. Well, as long as you are doing these activities strategically, rather than using them in order to avoid putting in the work, then you have my full permission to "slack" off every once in a while. It will make you happier, and help get you recovered so you can bring your A-Game the next time you play.

Mastery

Some of you might find it surprising that mastery would be considered a recovery experience.

A mastery experience is an activity in which you work to gain skills and improve performance in an area that is different from your main field of work. If you're not a professional player, this might even be what poker is for you! So, while these activities are challenging and require energy, the fact that you are growing, increasing skills, and entering into flow states means that you are improving mood, competence, and confidence, all of which lead to recovery.

There is also a detachment component here, given that these activities require focus and attention, you're less likely to dwell on poker or other work. Sports and exercise are excellent examples of this. When you approach your exercise as a mastery activity, rather than being just something you need to get done, you get the extra benefits that come with improvement and progression.

One of my favorite activities to insert here is martial arts, especially Brazilian Jiu Jitsu. The strategy aspect compliments poker nicely, and it goes a long way toward teaching you how to respectfully compete with your opponents. It's amazing how there can be so much camaraderie in a group of people who try to kill each other for a few hours each week. It's a good skill to have, as it allows you to go all out on the tables, without making it personal. Pair that with all the physical benefits, and you have pretty much the nuts when it comes to recovery activities.

It's not just sports and exercise that fit in here, anything where you're working towards mastery is great. It could be playing an instrument, learning a new language, art, fishing, pretty much whatever you can dream up will work. It's wise to find an activity that fits in with the core drivers that you discovered when you created your vision, and chances are you probably have a few activities in mind here that fit the mold.

Anytime you can find something that has complementary skills to poker but isn't directly poker related, you get the added benefit of adding those skills into your skill stack and recovering at the same time. Maybe this is taking a class on social skills or doing improv comedy if you're a live player, allowing you to better connect and extract information from your opponents. This is your chance to broaden your horizons while at the same time improving your performance on the tables.

Control

The fourth Recovery Experience cited by Sonnentag and Fritz is Control, which is a bit different than the rest as it's not so much a particular type of activity as it is a vital component of the activities that you choose. More accurately, the *fact* that you are choosing the activities you do is what matters.

Everyone has a desire to control the events in their life. Finding activities that fulfill this desire is even more important for poker players, who often won't get this sense of satisfaction from their work. When you're riding the swings of the game, it can be good to ground yourself with activities where it is very clear that you have control.

Here's a quote from that paper that demonstrates the importance of control:

"Personal control seems to be associated with positive reactions. It can lead to a positive reevaluation of potentially stressful situations and is associated with lower distress and higher psychological well being…"

Thus individual well-being increases when one feels in control of important life domains.

Now, this can play out in quite a few ways. This can come down to a feeling of control in your home life, and I certainly don't mean that in a negative way, where you're a controlling dictator telling everyone around you what to do. What it means is that you have stable relationships, where you know what to expect from those around you and they know what to expect from you.

So if you have relationships with family, partners, or friends that are volatile, you'll have an incredibly difficult time recovering. This is why it's important you surround yourself with quality people, who want the best for you in an honest and open way.

It can also mean having a stable financial situation. If you're unstable financially, recovery is very difficult. Not only will you feel pressure to play when you're not on your A-Game, but you'll be constantly thinking about how to come up with money or suffer the negative consequences of unpaid bills. This is another reason both bankroll and liferoll management is so important in poker. The game is volatile enough on its own. There's no need to add extra volatility by putting yourself in unstable situations.

A final way that control comes into play is actually choosing the leisure activities you participate in. This will mostly be an issue for those with families, but can also come into play when you have obligations outside of the game. If all your leisure activities are chosen by someone else, or on someone else's schedule, they won't take you very far in the recovery department. Make sure you set aside time that's just for you, and participate in some recovery exercises that you control.

Anti-Focus

One of the things I'm most known for is creating focus-boosting warm-up audios, which eventually turned into creating the Primed Mind app, so it might be a bit strange to hear me talk about something called anti-focus, but it's a tool that I've found to be incredibly powerful when it comes recovery.

So, what exactly do I mean when I say anti-focus? Well, it's quite literally the opposite of focus. It's time that you set aside to strategically let your mind wander in any direction it pleases. Focus is an important tool, there's no doubt that being highly focused is one of the biggest competitive edges you can have in today's world. So, yes focus is great, but focus in addition to anti-focus is even better.

For a highly driven person, it can be difficult to let go and just be with your own thoughts. There is a power in silence, a power in giving up control of your attention and letting your mind flow in whichever direction it pleases. A pattern that I've noticed in my high-performers is an extreme drive to improve themselves, which is obviously a great quality. The problem comes when it's taken a bit too far, where every down moment is filled with knowledge consumption. They notice feeling guilty if they aren't listening to a podcast, audio book, or training video during the little downtime that they have. Downtime starts to feel idle, even lazy, then used as an indicator that they are distancing themselves from success. Now, overall their mindset should be commended, and I certainly endorse using such resources to better yourself, but when you're constantly in consumption mode, constantly directing your attention and focus, you miss out on the opportunity to rest your mind and process the information you're learning.

Not only is anti-focus highly restorative, it is the time where your mind is at its most creative, you begin to harness the power of your imagination. When you're focused, you're attempting to find and follow the straightest, most efficient route to the outcome you're seeking. When you're anti-focused, your mind is reflecting, processing information in your subconscious, connecting new information with old, and using those connections to generate new, creative solutions to your problems.

If you've ever had a good idea or an "A-ha" moment pop up in the shower, this is why. You're in a relaxed state, not focused on anything in particular, and bang, you now understand how to solve that hand that's been bugging you for days.

You miss out on these moments, if you never give your mind the opportunity to anti-focus. A focused opponent is difficult to deal with. A focused and creative opponent is a force of nature that is nearly impossible to stop. That is what it means to be an A-Game Player.

So, what can you do to anti-focus in order to gain the creative and restorative benefits of this process? Well, first, start to establish comfort in your own thoughts. Find comfort with moments of emptiness. Set aside the need to fill every down moment with something that occupies and distracts your mind. The relaxation activities we talked about earlier are great examples of times where you can experience anti-focus. Simple, enjoyable activities in which you don't need to do much, if any, directed thinking.

Additionally, you can actually schedule anti-focus time on your calendar. Setting aside 15 to 20 minutes of journaling time each night can be a powerful way to process your day, plan for the future, and come up with creative solutions to your problems. Here, I'm talking about unstructured journaling where thoughts flow freely, rather than prompted journaling where you're answering the same few questions everyday.

My preferred method is to combine the two and have a few questions you ask yourself each night, as well as some time to just write down anything that comes to mind. Choose to schedule in some blocks of pure thinking time, where you plan to do nothing but sit around and think. It could be an hour every other week or 30 minutes four times a month, but blocking out pure thinking time can be one of the most powerful ways to upgrade your life.

Put yourself in an unstimulating room, and simply let your mind travel where it may. Or engage in an activity that doesn't require much thought, like washing dishes or a walk down a quiet road. You'll be amazed at what happens when you make this a habit, at just how quickly you work through the major problems that were previously stumping you.

Using long walks as thinking time is also a great option, just make sure you have your phone with you to take notes or voice recordings of any particular insights that you come up with along the way.

If there's an overwhelming problem in your life that is giving you particular trouble, dedicate an entire thinking time block to that single issue. Grab a pen and paper and start free flow writing about the issue. Write down everything that comes to mind and continue going for an amount of time you predetermine. If you don't come to a solution in 30 minutes or an hour, set it aside and do the same thing again tomorrow. Again, you'll be amazed at how quickly you work through it and change what seemed like an insoluble problem into a clear and simple plan of action. Your mind is a powerful tool. Make sure you put it to good use when problems arise.

Now, if you're feeling generally overwhelmed and flustered, but can't quite put your finger on the exact cause, do something that I call the 30-Minute Brain Dump. This means going to a quiet place where you won't be distracted, setting a timer for 30 minutes and writing down *everything* that comes to mind, *everything* you need to do, *everything* that's bothering you, and any problems you're facing. If you're 10 minutes in and can't think of anything, continue regardless. Just sit there thinking until the 30-minute timer is up. Usually what happens is people get 10 to 15 minutes in, think they have everything out, only to wait 5 minutes and get a massive dump of ideas for the last half of the exercise. After that 30 minutes, my guess is that most of the feelings of being overwhelmed and frustrated will be gone. Just getting it out of your head is powerful. You could even throw the paper away and see a benefit. But don't do that, because the info on that paper will be pure gold. It should give you a clear picture of the major roadblocks you need to work on, as well as ideas on how to break through them.

Anti-Focus is a powerful state of mind, and it's been an important breakthrough for many clients who were stuck in constant consumption mode. It's great to take in lots of information. You just need to make sure you have time to process it and actually give your mind the space to use that information for your benefit.

An advanced method for getting into a state of anti-focus is something called a sensory deprivation tank, also known as an isolation tank, or just a float tank. These tanks look like little mini-spaceship pods and are filled with salt water that is heated to your exact body temperature. That means when you lay in them, you float, and you don't feel the water, given that it's the same temperature as your skin. The pods are also sound proof and light blocking, blocking out most external stimulation. Essentially, the theory is that you're isolating your mind by removing light, sound and touch as you float weightlessly in the tank. In this state of weightless darkness, in which your entire being is made up of your thoughts and the sensation of your breath, you are able to experience one of the most powerful methods of anti-focus out there, great for relaxation, creativity, and visualization. With float centers popping up in almost every major city, it is a resource that is becoming ever more available and popular, and is something worth experimenting with if you're looking to take your anti-focus game to the next level. It's not something that everyone finds enjoyable, but those who do seem to really get some powerful benefits from that time alone with themselves.

Long-Term Breaks

So far, we've discussed recovering in micro moments during your session, taking short breaks while you play, and recovery in your daily and weekly schedule. Now, we want to take one step further back and look at your life on a monthly, quarterly, and yearly basis. Those who work a conventional job typically get anywhere from two to five weeks of pure vacation time from their job, in addition to holidays. Extended periods of recovery offer a powerful opportunity for growth.

Sadly, most poker players only take these extended breaks when they are forced to by burnout. They push push push, until they aren't able to push any more. Rather than waiting until you burnout and are forced to stop, let's work recovery activities into your yearly schedule, so that you can proactively recover, rather than attempt to do so reactively.

What are some of the activities you love to do but that aren't part of your day-to-day or week-to-week schedule? Do you want to travel a minimum of four weeks a year? Great, plan those trips well in advance, ideally to come directly after a time you know will be particularly draining.

If, for example, you know you're going to grind like crazy during the WSOP, you might want to plan a two- or three-week holiday directly after that. Traveling is a great way to gain a new perspective on the world, and a career in poker allows you the flexibility to take advantage of those experiences. If you're a professional player, traveling to play in a tournament series doesn't count, unless you're specifically booking time after the event that's just for recovery.

Travel is obviously the biggest thing that comes up with these longer-term recovery experiences, but it's not your only option. What matters is that you set aside some extended recovery periods, so that you can maintain A-Game Poker for the full year, not just a small portion of it. This, combined with all the other recovery strategies we've discussed, is how you become an A-Game Player for life, rather than a player who burns bright for a short period of time but whose game eventually fizzles out.

A-Game Exercise: Implementing Recovery Strategies

All right, we've covered an overview of recovery strategies. The next step is to work some recovery into your everyday life. Now that you understand the true power of recovery, it's time to get out your journal or document and decide where you'll start implementing it into your life.

Not doing so is depriving yourself of the full levels of performance you're capable of, and will hold you back from becoming a true A-Game Player.

By now, you should have some great strategies in place for your sleep routine. That's around 8 hours a day of recovery that's absolutely essential to high-performance.

Next, ask yourself this:

What will I do on a weekly basis to recover?

This is both activities you do everyday, a few times a week, or just once a week. My strong suggestion is that you take at least two days off from playing, and at least one day completely away from poker, study included. Most of my clients are on either a four- or five-playing days a week schedule. Even with a heavy study schedule added in, that leaves plenty of room to take at least one full day off. I would also either take a second full day completely off, or do a small study session in the morning of that second day, and then take the rest of the day off.

Once you've set aside that time you can fill it in whatever way is optimal for you, using examples from this chapter, or experimenting with other ideas that you might have. If you're not a professional poker player, this is a little different, as poker might be a mastery activity you use to recover from your conventional job. Even then, it's important to fit in some time that's not just work or poker. Poker is an incredibly taxing game, don't neglect to add in the relaxation and anti-focus strategies that we discussed.

Once you've taken the time to plan out the activities you'll use for recovery on a weekly basis, I want you to go into the schedule template you created earlier and specifically slot these into your template.

CHAPTER 27

YOU KNOW WHAT TO DO

If you've made it this far and completed the exercises in this section, you're well on your way to becoming an A-Game Player, and I'd like to take a moment to congratulate you. Go ahead, give yourself a nice good pat on the back. Most people will tell you that they want something more, but you've actually put in the time and effort to take action on doing so. That is something worth celebrating.

The path to becoming an A-Game player is not a complicated one. The strategies we've covered so far are not complex nor particularly groundbreaking. As I've said before, the difference between the best in the world and everyone else is not secret knowledge or hidden strategies. The difference is having a clear understanding of where you want to go, a systematic plan to get there, and the ability to consistently apply and iterate those systems.

Even before you picked up this book, I would wager that you had some level of understanding about what it takes to reach the highest levels of this game, or to be successful in other areas of your life. The question is:

"Why aren't you doing it?"

That is exactly the question we will answer in Part 4: What's Holding You Back? The A-Game Engine is a fantastic system for implementing the key strategies that create a successful poker player, however it's not the system that is the biggest reason why so many of my clients are so successful. At some level, we all understand what it takes to succeed. The hard part is taking those actions consistently. The strategies are not complicated, but that does not mean they are easy to implement. Knowing what to do, and actually doing it are two very different things. It's the difference between becoming one of the best in the world and being in the middle of the pack.

The reason that I've been so successful in my career as a performance coach, is because I'm able to help my clients go from knowing to doing. To overcome the invisible resistance that prevents them from taking the actions they know they must take to succeed. Answering the Fundamental Performance Question is just the first step. What's next is discovering the reasons you aren't already matching the actions and efforts of those who are most successful in the area you're looking to succeed in.

This is the most fascinating part of the journey, and the one where you'll need to be the most introspective and honest with yourself. So, if you've ever felt like there was an invisible force field holding you back from reaching your full potential, stick with me. In part 4, we dive into "What's Holding You Back" and turn all the knowledge we've acquired so far into something you consistently apply both on and off the tables.

PART 4

What's Holding You Back?

I started working with Elliot to improve my bankroll management and emotional stability when playing for very high stakes. The early sessions working through my past had a huge impact on my poker and direction in life.

Surprisingly, the most value came from the work we've done after those issues were resolved. I've become a more successful poker player, and a better father, friend and husband. Knowing I have someone on hand to help me resolve any problem is invaluable, which is why I've worked with Elliot for 6 years and have no plans to stop.

-Chalie Hook - High-Stakes Cash Game Player

Chapter 28

The Four Performance Roadblocks

Why did you buy this book? Maybe you were just curious about learning more about my methods based on the big-name poker players I work with. My guess is that most of you who are reading this book have one thing in common: You want something more.

What that means varies from person to person, but if you were completely comfortable and content with where you are right now in the game and in life, you wouldn't be reading. And that begs the question:

What's Holding You Back?

Is that a question you've asked yourself before? The likelihood, given that you're here, is that there's something. I mean, let's face it. If you were already on the perfect path to achieving everything you'd ever desired, you wouldn't still be looking for guidance. Now, please don't take that as a negative. In fact, it's the exact opposite.

I've worked with a lot of incredibly successful people in poker, business, and athletics, and I've yet to meet anyone who didn't have something holding them back from becoming the best version of themselves.

In fact, the awareness of these roadblocks and the drive to constantly improve is what makes them so successful.

So, before we go any further, I ask you to acknowledge:

1) That you want something more from poker and life.
2) That there are roadblocks currently holding you back from getting there.
3) That you embrace these as truths and see those roadblocks as opportunities to improve, rather than as negative character traits.

Once you do that, you'll be available for an instant mindset shift where you go from struggling to acknowledge what's holding you back, to seeing your roadblocks as exciting challenges for you to tackle each day. And with that we can get started on identifying and eliminating these obstacles. Previously, we've answered the first part of the Fundamental Performance Question:

"What are the best in the world doing that I'm not?"

In this section, we tackle the "I'm not" part of the question and discover what's holding you back from doing so. If you're not achieving the success you want in poker, or any area of your life, it probably boils down to these simple reasons:

1) You don't *know* what to do to get there,

2) You know what to do but *can't,*

3) You know what to do but *won't.*

When you break these reasons down, they lead into what I call: *The Four Performance Roadblocks*

If you ask a random sampling of people on the street what it takes to become a successful poker player, you'll likely get some hilarious answers. It's doubtful, however, that any of them will be able to tell you anything of real value. They certainly won't be able to give you an actionable step-by-step plan you can implement over the next 6 months, year, or five years to achieve that goal. In fact, they probably wouldn't even come close to painting a picture of what I described in the "Anatomy of an A-Game Player" section. Their lack of understanding of the game means they have no vision of a successful poker player. Not knowing where you're going makes it incredibly difficult to achieve anything. Without a plan, a map, or a path, it's nearly impossible to make any meaningful progress. Before you can achieve success, you need to have at least a rough idea of what success looks like, and an idea of how to get there. This means that lack of vision is Performance Roadblock Number 1.

After we know *what* to do (meaning we have a *vision* and a *plan*) we need to actually do it. The second reason for the lack of success I mentioned was: You know *what* to do but *can't*.

The two main reasons for this are either that you don't have the ability to take necessary actions, or you don't have energy needed to take them.

Let's take one of those random people we interviewed on the streets earlier, put them in a room with Fedor Holz, and have Fedor explain everything he did to become one of the best poker players in the world and what he does to maintain that status. That would be a great start (comparing what you do to what the best in the world do is a great place to start when it comes to vision), but that random person wouldn't walk out of that room as a successful player themselves. They would still need to acquire the necessary skills to follow through with that plan. That makes lack of skill Performance Roadblock Number 2.

Now, let's jump a year into the future. Fedor took that random person under his wing, trained them day in and day out, and turned him into a new mini-Fedor 2.0, with a crystal-clear vision and plenty of skill. Now, we keep that player up for three days straight with no food and put them in a game. Would that player be able to perform? Certainly not. They know *what* to do, but they *can't* because they lack the energy to perform. Obviously, an extreme example, but I'm sure you can relate to this one. Poor focus, burnout, C-Game play—all are connected with energy. That makes lack of energy Performance Roadblock Number 3.

Now this is where things start to get interesting. The final reason I gave was that you know what to do but won't. You have the vision, you have the skill, you have the energy, but you won't perform. You might be saying...

"Hey Elliot, if I know exactly what I need to do, have the skill to do it, and the energy I need to execute it, why in the world would I choose not to?"

That's certainly a good question, and logically speaking it's not something that *should* happen. Yet it does.

ALL. THE. TIME.

Ever make a play at the table you specifically knew was wrong? Ever fail to take a risk that you knew was correct, out of fear of failing and looking silly? Yeah, logically when we know what to do, we should do it. But humans are far from purely logical creatures. If we were, I would be out of a job and this book wouldn't exist. I've seen studies where 70% or more of patients coming off a major cardiovascular episode fail to comply with the recommendation of their doctor. It doesn't get any more illogical than someone failing to follow through in a situation where you are told to change or die, but it happens all the time. Why is this?

Well, it's the fourth Performance Roadblock, what I call Detrimental Mental Programs.

We shouldn't start slamming our chips out of frustration after we get a bad beat and then playing recklessly, but it happens all the time. We shouldn't start to self-sabotage when things finally start to go well, but it happens all the time. We shouldn't take lots of actions that feel good in the moment, but don't serve our long-term goals. But we do.

And it's because when we come across a decision that conflicts with what we consciously know we should do and what our Mental Program wants us to do, the subconscious programming usually wins.

So, there you have it, the Four Performance Roadblocks.

Lack Of Vision

Lack Of Skill

Lack Of Energy

Detrimental Mental Programs

I believe the reason that so many of my private clients have had such success is because the first thing we do is address these Detrimental Mental Programs. In fact, when I first got started working in the performance coaching industry, that was pretty much my sole focus.

Using hypnosis, I'll work with my client's subconscious to identify these mental programs and then change them into something that moves them forward, rather than holds them back.

Once those major Performance Roadblocks are lifted, we'll start to build on our now solid foundation, and effectively apply all the other "A-Game" strategies and tactics we cover in the rest of this book.

CHAPTER 29

DETRIMENTAL MENTAL PROGRAMS

Where do Detrimental Mental Programs come from, and why do they exist in the first place?

To get to an answer, we have to first understand the distinction between the conscious and the subconscious mind. The conscious mind is the part of our mind we are actively aware of. The subconscious or unconscious mind is the operating system that runs everything else in the background. The amount of information and functions we need to run simultaneously is massive, and we would absolutely freeze up if we had to consciously think about every little detail and decision we needed to make. Just think about the simple act of standing up from a chair. You don't consciously think:

"All right, feet, flex up from the toe joints while applying downward force to lift up as thigh and knees muscles contract simultaneously, and at the same time keep breathing with heart pumping, etc., etc..."

Of course, the actual complexity of the action is way greater than my rough example, and in reality you just think "Stand up," and your subconscious handles the rest. When you throw in all other physical attributes a human body calls upon throughout the course of a day, including environmental awareness, predictive analysis, and social interaction, you begin to see the complexity of what we are dealing with here. Which brings me to my first major point:

The subconscious mind is here to help.

It's here to help us function, to help us survive, and to protect us. This is an important fact to remember because it's not always obvious. Your conscious and subconscious mind are both on "Team You." They just don't always agree on what's best for you. Without your subconscious mental programs, you simply would not be able to function.

A mental program becomes detrimental when the situation that the program was designed to protect you from no longer exists or was based on a false premise or signal in the first place, or when your subconscious mistakenly categorizes something as dangerous when it really isn't.

Most of our programming occurs in childhood. When we come into this world, we have a long way to go before we can function in society, even on the most basic level. We learn the majority of what we need to know through observation, modeling, and trial and error. Young minds are sponges that soak up and learn all the complexities of existence that are essential to human survival. We need to learn how to use our bodies, how to use our minds, how to interact socially, all of this information stored in the "Mental Programs" embedded in our subconscious. There is no book we can pick up to read that tells us the best way to be human, we absorb that information from our environment. We learn what's "good" and "bad," "right" and "wrong," "dangerous" and "safe." And here's the thing:

We don't always get the correct and most beneficial data from our environment. Sometimes we create programs in order to protect us - from our parents, trauma, various foods, even from our peers. A young child is completely dependent on their parents, so it's a simple survival mechanism to create mental programs that are in line with what the parents and elders believe and how they act. Once a child hits school age, teachers and peers become a major influence, so we create mental programs designed to help us survive and manage those environments.

It may seem that "protect" and "survive" are heavy terms, but that's how the subconscious mind sees it. It's quite common for our subconscious to have created programs that don't actually serve to improve our lives after we have matured out of a significantly more vulnerable childhood.Early incidents, confrontations, and encounters that might seem minor to an outside observer, can have a ripple effect on the individual that lasts a lifetime.

This is obviously a subject where science is always evolving, and we are still many years away from fully understanding how the mind works, if we ever do. However, this should give you the foundational understanding of the basics and allow you to start to understand where your mental programs come from, and why they don't always serve the purpose of protecting you.

For starters, let's take a look at some examples of Detrimental Mental Programs, and see how they can cause issues for a poker player. A simple example might be a mental program that said:

Poker is a Game of Pure Luck

If you had this program running, you wouldn't even think of attempting to become a serious poker player. Obviously, that would be a huge roadblock to poker performance. You might play the game for fun just like someone would play a slot machine, but the idea of putting work into improving your game would never cross your mind. Since you're reading this book, however, I'm fairly certain that won't be the case for you. Still, it's not an all or nothing proposition. Many of you will have friends and family who think poker is all luck and aren't shy about communicating that. Even if you consciously know otherwise, it can still start to seep into your subconscious. Mix that with an extended downswing and you could find yourself avoiding putting in any meaningful work because…

"It's all luck anyways."

Another Detrimental Mental Program that I often see is one that says:

Money is Bad and so Are People Who Have It

Imagine you put in a ton of work and finally start earning an amount that puts you head and shoulders above what you're used to seeing in your life. You grew up in a family without a lot of money, and your parents constantly told you how money was the root of all evil and shared stories that vilified the rich. How did this message infiltrate your consciousness? Well, for many players this is where self-sabotage comes in. Think of it like an internal money thermostat. You make an amount of money that you feel is acceptable to earn, so you're okay putting in the work to reach that level, but if you find yourself making more than that, you always manage to find a way to bring it back down to your comfort zone.

Another Detrimental Mental Program that's quite common and can be a massive roadblock to poker success:

I'm Just Not a Math Person

If you had parents or teachers who often said things like:

"We just aren't good at math in our family."

"It's okay, you're just not a math person."

The idea might become part of a program that runs every time you come upon a difficult math problem. Rather than the logical approach of:

"This is a difficult math problem, let me try to figure it out."

You immediately default to:

"I'm not a math person," and give up without even trying.

An idea that probably has little actual substance, quickly becomes a self-fulfilling prophecy based on your programming. Obviously, understanding the math side of the game is crucial to succeeding these days, so if you just brush it off completely, you diminish your chance of success greatly. The alternative requires that you stand in absolute opposition of an identity assigned to you, and maybe generations before you. Take a moment to think about all the actions we covered in The Anatomy of An A-Game Player. At the end of the section, we asked the question:

"Why Am I Not Already Doing All of These Things?"

If you know that you should be taking an action to achieve your goals, but you aren't, that's a telltale sign that you have a Detrimental Mental Program unconsciously blocking the action. I hope that you are able to read these stories and understand this is a process all A-Game Players must go through, whether they do it with a performance coach or are able to work it out on their own.

CHAPTER 30

DETRIMENTAL MENTAL PROGRAM EXAMPLES

I've worked with poker players as a performance coach for over a decade. Many of them you'll recognize as being among the best players in the world. Others you would know except they've chosen to remain anonymous. What they all have in common is that each and every one of them had a buildup of Detrimental Mental Programs that we were able to unravel during our time working together. In this chapter, I'm going to go through a wide range of the most common Detrimental Mental Programs I've seen in them. Too often we only see the tournament winners' trophies or pictures of massive chip stacks without knowing what it took for those players to get to that point. I can tell you that nobody who made it to the top had an easy journey.

I'd also like to say how much it means to me that the players you'll meet in this chapter were so open in talking about the roadblocks they dealt with. I think it's invaluable to get a sense of what the best of the best had to go through to get to where they are.

While I've been able to classify the most common Detrimental Mental Programs that repeat themselves for the majority of poker players, I want to emphasize that every Detrimental Mental Program is unique to each individual, and all of them have different life experiences that have shaped them in their unique journey through the world.

To be sure, there are commonalities and overlap in the types of Detrimental Mental Programs, and how yours was formed and how it affects you will be different than how they formed for Phil Galfond, Fedor Holz, Jason Koon, and all the other professionals featured in this chapter.

The goal here is to gain insight into the many ways our past programming affects our current performance,thus creating the space for introspection concerning the areas that are holding you back from becoming an A-Game Player.

Here's how we're going to accomplish that. For each Detrimental Mental Program I'll share:

How It Shows,

How It Hurts,

How It Serves,

Where It Starts.

The third one is critical, and I want you to pay extra attention to it. These mental programs are designed to serve you in some way, and there is almost always some form of secondary gain for running a program that might otherwise feel completely destructive and illogical. Understanding how the Detrimental Mental Program serves you is the genesis for starting to resolve the issue. Realizing that your subconscious has your best interests in mind is essential to being able to accept and resolve that roadblock. And this is true even when it feels complete at odds with the goals and ambitions you have for poker and life.

As you read these examples and stories, take note of situations that sound familiar to your situation. While every person is unique, knowing where to start will give you a leg up when it comes to working with a performance coach or trying to address these Detrimental Mental Programs in another way. With that, let's get started.

Too Smart to Try

How It Shows

Players with the *Too Smart to Try* program running, attempt to succeed in poker based purely on their raw intelligence. Instead of taking advantage of all the resources available for studying the game, they use their own internal processing methods to work on improving. They don't like to read books, watch training videos, or use solvers. They may even avoid talking much poker with other players, as they don't want other people's thoughts and ideas to influence their own. Typically, this type of player is quite intelligent, and their early success and rapid ascent in the game often further fortifies this program.

How it Hurts

As we discussed in the Evolution of a Winning Poker Player chapter, it is extremely difficult, and almost impossible to reach the top of the game based on intelligence alone. The theory and technology continue to evolve at too fast a pace for anyone other than an actual genius to keep up. Even for those who do possess that level of elite intelligence, the failure to take advantage of every resource available to them unnecessarily hamstrings their progress.

How it Serves

Too Smart to Try is a program designed for ego protection. The subconscious mind has built up an image of who this player is, and their worth is directly correlated with their intelligence. By trying, and giving 100 percent of their effort, they risk failing and shattering that ideal version of themselves. If you never try, and never give it all you can, you can always look back and say, "I would have been successful if I'd really tried."

Where it Starts

This program starts with someone who has above average intelligence and is told so, and even praised, by those around them. While that may seem harmless on the surface, and even something that could be viewed as a positive, the problem comes when that intelligence is not challenged, which is incredibly common in the school system. Assignments, grades, and test scores come easy, and these individuals are never forced to put in extra work or struggle to find a solution. They learn to view their intelligence as an innate personality trait, not something that they need to work hard to improve or maintain.

When that trait gets closely tied to their self-worth, the subconscious creates a program to avoid any situation that might call their intelligence into question. Failure is no longer viewed as an opportunity for growth, but as a risk to their identity and value as a human.

PRO CASE STUDY

PHIL GALFOND

HIGH-STAKES PROFESSIONAL & FOUNDER OF RUN IT ONCE POKER

For years, I succeeded at the highest levels of poker, putting in very little time studying off the table. Back then, people were not studying the way they do today, and my ability to adjust to my opponents faster than they adjusted to me gave me a significant edge in the games.

Eventually, I launched a couple of businesses, and my responsibilities there pulled me away from playing the game full time and at the highest levels. I started to think of myself as a businessman instead of a poker player, with my play being limited to making training videos and the occasional big tournament event. I attended one of Elliot's Mastermind events in Vegas, and shared with the group that I wasn't happy with the direction my career was going. The businesses were doing well, but I was struggling to find the same passion for business that I had when I was playing poker full time. The question was posed to me:

"What if being one of the best players in the world and playing the highest stakes is how you could add the most value to your company?"

I knew I loved playing poker, but I was telling myself that I was a businessman now, and that needed to be my focus. With this new perspective it sounded like I could have the best of both worlds, so I knew I needed to give it a shot.

The problem was, I'd missed out on five years of growth in the game, which is like missing multiple decades in other industries. Solvers had taken over the game, and I had a strong suspicion that I couldn't hang with the solver kids and that what made me great before was no longer a viable edge. I feared that I couldn't hang with the best and didn't want to go from being a nosebleed winner considered to be one of the best in the world to just being good enough to beat 5-10 or 10-20 online, but no higher. This fear was keeping me from jumping back in, so even though I wanted to do it, I kept putting it off to an indeterminate time in the future.

Eventually, I took Elliot's A-Game Poker Masterclass. One of the exercises he had us go through was called B.R.A.V.E. The exercise had me list my biggest fear, which was around fully applying myself to studying solvers. Then it had me list the worst-case scenario if I faced this fear, which was going all-in on solvers and not being able to process and execute on the information I learned. From there, I realized that even if this happened, I still had great options. I could work with a coach or try a different approach. Even if I failed completely, I would still be in the same spot as I already was, no worse off than if I didn't try at all. At that point I had already sort of given up on the idea of high-stakes poker, so really there was nothing tangible to fear, the worst-case scenario was that I just would end up right back where I started.

That's when I started working with Elliot one-on-one to break through the subconscious side of the fears, now that I consciously knew the real-world risk was essentially zero.

Through that private coaching, I discovered I was running a "Too Smart to Try" program. From a very early age I was constantly told how smart I was. School came easy to me, and that ease became a part of my identity. I expected and needed to be good at whatever I was doing, without much effort. Around eighth grade, I began avoiding any situations that challenged that identity. I stopped studying and doing my homework and was still able to maintain myself as a B student, telling myself that if I really wanted to, I could try hard and be at the top of my class. By never pushing myself, I never had to find out I wasn't the best or that I wasn't as smart as I thought I was. That carried over to poker.

I was lucky that I came up when I did. At the time the strategic side of the game wasn't as evolved as it is now. My ability to internally synthesize information and adjust to my opponent's game gave me a big edge. Had I come up in today's game, with the same approach and mindset I wouldn't have made it.

So, when it came time to get back into the game, we knew that I had to take a different approach. It wasn't about throwing away all the attributes that had allowed me to be successful early on, it was about merging those skills and abilities with the reality of how you need to study to play the modern game. I needed to test myself in certain areas even if that meant risking my identity as the naturally gifted smart kid.

That's where the idea of The Galfond Challenge came from. Playing poker is my biggest passion, yet I still had responsibilities with my business. We have so many talented and capable people working behind the scenes. My role in the company was replaceable, likely with someone who could do the same job even better that I could. But I was the only one who could get on the tables and be me. The challenge checked all the boxes. I could play the game I loved, promote the business, and finally test myself again and face the fears Elliot and I uncovered doing all this mindset work.

The first challenge was against Venivedi, one of the top regs at high-stakes PLO. We were set to play 25,000 hands at 100/200, with a 20k buy-in. The winner would also claim an additional $100,000 as a side bet. I was looking to test myself, and right out of the gate it looked like that test was going to be a fail. In the first 9000 hands I was down 45 buy-ins, just around $900,000. I continued to work with Elliot the whole time, keeping my head on straight as I was playing.

Despite the results I was happy with my play and, given how I was running, it could have been a lot worse if I hadn't been doing that work. I took a two-week break to evaluate the situation and decide if I wanted to concede the challenge (and pay out the extra $100,000) or keep playing on. At the start of the break most people expected me to quit, and the truth is, that was the way I was leaning, *myself. However, after some analysis, I was confident in my play, and more important, not ready to give up on myself. My analysis told me I could hang with him, and I wanted to prove to myself that I could execute.*

I decided to give it a shot and continue. I didn't have any expectations of winning, but wanted to play my best and hopefully win back five or ten buy-ins through the final 16,000 hands. What ended up happening was better than I could have imagined: a miraculous comeback all the way to making back the 45 buy-ins and winning the challenge by a hair on the final day. It was really a ridiculous run and felt like something straight from a movie script.

Since then, I've gone on to win a few more challenges in much less dramatic fashion. Not only was this a big win for the business, but it's also been invaluable for my personal happiness. I now get to play poker at the highest level, after facing my biggest fears head on and proving to myself I could do it.

Career-wise, all the work I've done with Elliot has been massive, but more important, for my personal happiness, it's been a very big turning point in my life.

Hide Your Shine

How it Shows

Hide Your Shine is a Detrimental Mental Program designed to mask your positive attributes, typically intelligence or skill when it comes to poker. Players with this program try to stay in the background, even when it means sacrificing profits. This often shows up in live MTTs when players are closing in on a highly publicized final table or are on a featured table.

It can also show up as a lack of giving full effort or putting a strong effort into study. The subconscious knows that these activities lead to success, and this program views success as recognition, which it desperately wants to avoid.

How it Hurts

The most obvious way *Hide Your Shine* hurts your profitability is by forcing suboptimal play in situations where winning would bring unwanted attention.

The less obvious way it hurts your profitability is by putting up roadblocks to success in general, stopping you from taking the actions that make an A-Game Player successful.

How it Serves

This is a clear example of how a subconscious program and a conscious desire can be in direct conflict with each other.

Your conscious brain would love to ship a massive tournament, while your subconscious brain understands hitting a huge score, and all the attention that comes with it, as a massive negative.

Where it Starts

Hide Your Shine is created when family members, teachers, or peers "take you down a peg" whenever you are excited about an achievement.

In school, kids are often bullied for being "too smart" as peers try to bring the other kids down to their level.

Parents and teachers can also be afraid of children who excel, letting their own Detrimental Mental Programs affect how they treat such children.

Pro Case Study

Fedor Holz

High-Stakes MTT Professional with Over $40,000,000 in Live Earnings

In poker, things aren't always as they appear.

In September 2014, I won the WCOOP Main Event for $1,300,000. After that, I hit the High Roller circuit and cashed for $372,208 and $369,152 in Monte Carlo. At the WSOP, I placed 3rd in the 10k Six Max for $268,463. To cap it off, I made a deep run in the Main Event, placing 25th for $262,574.

From the outside, it looked like I was on top of the poker world. However, when I busted the Main Event, I went back to my hotel room and cried over poker for the first time ever. While it looked like things were going well from the outside, between the WCOOP Main event win and the WSOP Main Event, I lost around $600,000, or about 40% of my bankroll.

In poker, everyone sees the cashes, but cashes aren't profits. Between having only a small piece of myself in the High-Rollers, to playing nearly every tournament on the slate, what looked like a great post-WCOOP run, really felt like a disaster. The worst part was, I had nobody to talk to about my struggles. When it looks like you're winning everything, poker players have a hard time caring about your problems, especially when they haven't had scores anywhere close to yours.

That's why when I went from a big stack against a super soft field in the Main Event, to out in 25th in just a few hours, I was devastated. First place was $10,000,000 and I had 60% of myself, so

$250,000 felt like an insult with how I'd been running for the last six months. Back in the hotel room there were fleeting thoughts of quitting the game, or busting my roll. Thankfully, I did neither.

A few months later, I started working with Elliot. I had heard good things about his coaching and actually purchased a session for a friend as a birthday present. His review was so good that I decided to give it a chance myself.

From the very first session, I understood why so many high-level players wanted to work with Elliot. We quickly discovered that I was running a subconscious program he calls, "Hide Your Shine." Elliot discovered that I had been capping myself, not allowing myself to play full out. We tied this back to my school days, where I was bullied for my intelligence and drive. I started holding back, never wanting to show my full potential, because that was the safe thing to do.

Two weeks after I started with Elliot, I played the $25,000 WSOPE in Berlin, and made the final table. I was third out of six, and the table was full of excellent, well-known players. I got there 15 minutes early and listened to the mindset MP3 Elliot had recorded for me. I was absolutely in the zone. It felt like the rest of the world was moving half as fast as usual. I felt great, maybe the best I had ever felt at a live final table up to that point.

…And then I busted the fifth hand in.

This next part I will never forget. I stood up, smiled to myself, and was certain that from there on out I would just focus on playing great. Good results, bad results, I felt like I could control my experience. That was mind-blowing.

After that I went all-in with Elliot and the mental side of the game. I remember a particular session, preparing for the Alpha 8, a

$100,000 buy-in, at the Bellagio. It was a particularly emotional session, and I remember at the end, saying,

"I'm just going to win now."

We had done a ton of work on me unblocking myself so that I could show my full potential, and in that moment I was staking my claim. I knew I was going to go out and give everything I had. The next eight months went better than I ever could have imagined.

Here are the highlights of that run:

$100,000 Alpha 8 - 1st - $1,589,219

$200,000 Triton Super High-Roller Series - 1st - $3,072,748

$10,000 EPT Monte Carlo - 4th - $190,122

$50,00 EPT Monte Carol - 5th - $310,892

$300,000 Super High-Roller Bowl - 2nd - $3,500,000

$50,000 Aria Super High-Roller - 1st - $637,392

$25,000 Aria Super High-Roller - 1st - $393,120

$25,000 Aria Super High-Roller - 1st - $276,012

$50,000 Aria Super High-Roller - 3rd - $407,310

$111,111 WSOP High-Roller for One Drop - 1st - $4,981,775

$25,000 EPT Barcelona - 1st - $1,473,127

In the first year of working with Elliot and focusing on A-Game Poker, I went from my lowest moment in the game to cashing for over $15,000,000 and winning my first WSOP bracelet. It's hard to put into words the impact that working with Elliot has had. Obviously, the money and the trophies are amazing. However, the confidence of knowing what I am capable of doing when I no longer hold myself back is priceless. That's why I've continued to work with Elliot on a

> *near weekly basis for the last seven years, and have no plans to slow down.*

The Bigger Bully

How It Shows

The Bigger Bully is a program that shows itself through reckless aggression and unnecessary conflicts.

When a player becomes aggressive against you, rather than looking at the situation as a puzzle that must be solved, you take it personally and fire right back at them, even if it's a suboptimal play. If your opponent is an A-Game Player, and isn't taking the "battle" personally, you become an easy target as you allow your emotions to dictate your play, rather than strategy.

This also presents when you go out of your way to battle tough opponents for personal rather than strategic reasons. You need to be the best in your game and do whatever it takes to prove it.

How It Hurts

Anytime you're making decisions based on emotions over strategy, you're not playing A-Game Poker. MTT players with this program will unnecessarily bust huge stacks going after other strong players whom they feel are bullying them. Cash game players will find themselves with weak holdings in a massive pot due to ill-timed aggression, then try to bluff their way out of the situation, only to be easily picked off by a more level-headed player.

How It Serves

Many programs are created from being bullied as a child. You may have felt powerless back then, but poker gives you the opportunity to fight back against bullies and get some of that power back.

The only problem is that there really isn't such a thing as a bully in poker. The notion of a big stack "picking" on a small stack is in fact giving an emotional characterization to what should rather be seen as optimal strategic play. In a case like that, for example, your opponent with the big stack is making "aggressive" plays, and you, with your small stack, are getting the fair opportunity to counter his plays. Your decisions need to separate emotional language from describing what should be seen as the best correct move.

When *The Bigger Bully* program operates in your subconscious, it seeks to inject a powerful sense of compensation for the inner helplessness that is triggered.

Where It Starts

This program is almost always linked to childhood bullying. As you'll see in the story that follows, sometimes the child may have started fighting back and decided they would be the bully instead of letting others do it for them. This can also show up in other situations where you felt powerless with authority figures, and now poker provides an opportunity to make up for that feeling.

PRO CASE STUDY

JON VAN FLEET

HIGH-STAKES MTT PROFESSIONAL WITH OVER $22,000,000 IN ONLINE EARNINGS

When I started working with Elliot I already had a decade plus of beating up high-stakes online MTTs under my belt. Staying at the top of the game for so long is no easy feat, and I'm incredibly proud of my ability to adjust my game to keep up with an ever-changing strategic poker landscape.

Early on, a poker coach suggested I keep a journal to get awareness around what could be tripping me up in-game, and what events kept repeating. Something that kept coming up was that when anyone would 3-bet me a few times in a row, I would emotionally 4-bet all-in pre-flop. While 4-betting "light" with good reason is okay occasionally, in these instances all strategic thought went out the window and I would play back at them with any two cards and a whole bunch of rage.

I wasn't able to solve this issue through my normal strategic process, because it wasn't a strategic problem. I knew the proper ranges to play back at them, but when it felt like I was getting bullied, I saw red and let my rage take over. Eventually this really started to damage my results, so I sought out Elliot to help me fix this issue. Right away, Elliot called out something that has stuck with me ever since.

"If someone 3-bets you more than once, they can pretty much get your stack."

That really stung because I realized how easy it was for my opponents to trigger me emotionally and take advantage of me after.

During one of our sessions, Elliot asked me to remember the first time that I felt this rage. It was when I was when I moved from California to Texas. I was the new kid in school. I don't know what my mom was thinking, but I had these hot pink shoelaces and a San Francisco Forty-Niners jacket in Texas, and I wore them to school every day and got bullied. Mostly verbally bullied, as I was a pretty big kid. It seemed like nobody liked me. I'd never felt such rejection. I came home from school everyday, crying. And then I realized one day that I was bigger than those kids and I started fighting back, physically. Once I got over that initial new kid phase, I got my own group of friends. After that, I started to look for bullies to beat up.

In high school, I specifically remember looking for people who were picking on other people, so I could pick on them. I thought I was justified. I thought I was the good guy, but I was really just using the hero persona as an excuse to beat kids up. I was masking my insecurities by trying to be the bigger bully. Elliot and I went deep into that feeling and got into the emotions behind it. During the session Elliot said:

"So, now that you've let that emotion go? Are you really going to let eight-year-old Jon make decisions at the poker table?"

It was like a lightbulb went off. And now, every time I get 3-bet and that feeling starts rising up, I just remember that it's my eight-year-old self and that helps me become aware and process the situation. And maybe I will 4-bet in their eye, but it'll be because I have good strategic reasons, not because I'm pissed off.

Too Much of a Good Thing

How it Shows

Have you ever had everything go incredibly well, only to get the feeling that what was happening was too good to be true, and you were left waiting for the other shoe to drop? When the *Too Much of a Good Thing* program runs, you're not waiting for that other shoe to drop, you're subconsciously finding ways to bring it down.

Maybe things are going exceedingly well in your personal life, and you start to have a bad run at poker. Maybe you're playing great poker, and notice you're starting fights with your significant other, or starting to skip out on your health and wellness routines.

And, of course, many who have this program running will achieve a certain level of success at the tables and continue to find new and creative ways to drop those successful results back down to a level where they feel subconsciously comfortable.

How it Hurts

This program doesn't prevent you from being successful, but it applies a very narrow window of what that success is allowed to look like. With *Too Much of a Good Thing* running, too much success is often viewed as more painful than having too little.

A-Game Players squeeze out as much profit potential as they can from the talents and abilities they have. *Too Much of a Good Thing* creates a success ceiling and, once you surpass it, it will crash and burn whatever it can to get you back into its comfort zone. This means you cap your success and aren't able to take advantage of the compound growth that can be achieved by consistently performing at a high level in the game.

Please note that I did not say "your comfort zone." If you have this program (or something similar) and I ask you what your desired level of success is, you'll likely say much higher than it is now. This is why I say that it's the program's comfort zone, because, as we say, when a conscious desire and a subconscious program conflict, the subconscious program almost always comes out on top.

How it Serves

The goal of the subconscious is to protect you. If you have a belief, consciously or unconsciously, that "More Success = More Problems," then too much of that good thing suddenly becomes a major problem. What you consciously feel to be a fantastic result is seen as a mortal threat by this program, and the self-sabotage that results is like releasing the pressure from a valve that's dangerously close to exploding.

Where It Starts

At some point your subconscious decided that there was a certain level of success that it deemed safe and tolerable. Maybe you had a family member who was incredibly successful and had it all fall apart. Rather than examining the root cause of that failure, you made a connection that said "Big Success = Pain" and started running it in the background. Maybe your family had a comfortable middle-class life and made offhand remarks about successful individuals. Things like:

"I would never want to have that much money; all it does is create more problems."

"No good ever came from being so successful; you have to sell your soul to get there and end up becoming a terrible person."

"It's like the more money we come across, the more problems that we see."

There can also be a self-worth component to *Too Much of a Good Thing*. If you believe you're not a person who deserves or has earned X amount of success, then you'll find ways to tear yourself down once you've crossed that threshold.

Back Against the Wall

How it Shows

A player with the *Back Against the Wall* program needs to feel an extreme amount of pressure in order to perform at their best. You'll often see this type of player get stuck early in a cash game session before they finally start to play their A-Game.

These players will go from massive bankroll to stone broke, then run it back up again, only to burn it all down and begin the cycle all over. Players running this program find all sorts of ways to make the game harder than it needs to be. Maybe it's playing in tough games at stakes their bankroll can't really tolerate. Maybe it's not studying or neglecting to pick up on other player's tendencies as a way to keep the challenge level as high as possible. Players with this program need an antagonist—be it a person or a situation—in order to unlock their best game.

How it Hurts

The simple formula for poker success is to find spots where you have a large edge and avoid spots where your edge is the smallest. *Back Against the Wall* players throw this out the window.

While it's true these players often perform extremely well under pressure, continually putting yourself in a losing position isn't a winning formula even if you're the best in the world. If, instead of always having to play from behind, these players could just unlock the ability to perform when things were going well, they'd be able to skip the whole "Crash, Burn, Rebuild" cycle and continue to climb continuously.

How it Serves

Poker is a highly competitive game, and this program tells you that the only way you can be at your best is when your back is against the wall. The truth is, coming out on top when the odds are stacked against you does feel good. For most players, winning a buy-in after being stuck five will feel so much more satisfying than winning a buy-in by chipping away at small pots for the whole night.

Being "In the Zone," completely locked in, feels fantastic, and if you believe that you can only access this state when you're in a tough spot, you'll end up seeking out that feeling, even if the way you go about getting there is completely counter to your consciously stated goals. There are countless examples of players who go from multi-million-dollar bankrolls to broke, and then back up to seven-figures again. These players often become folk heroes in the poker world. Sadly, this type of player almost always flames out because the big comeback style is too hard to sustain.

Where it Starts

This program typically starts as a program stacked on top of another program. There's another program running that prevents them from taking action until the very last minute, and they succeed only because their back is against the wall. As this pattern repeats, the program is reinforced until they feel like the only way they're able to perform is when they have an extreme amount of pressure placed on them. Performing well under pressure can be a superpower, but it can also become a major crutch when it feels like the only way you can perform is with the weight of the world on your shoulders.

Never Lucky

How it Shows

Players running the *Never Lucky* program view the world through the glass half-empty lens. They feel like they are the unluckiest player in the game and take every opportunity to let you know it. Their bluffs fail because they *always* run into the top of their opponent's ranges. Their call-downs fail because their opponents' *always have it.* They lose flips in *every* big spot, and their aces get cracked in the absolute worst spots.

How it Hurts

When you view your success and failures as the product of luck, you tend to miss opportunities to put in the work needed to control your outcomes. What's the point of studying if it's all luck anyways? You don't need to review your bluffs when you just got unlucky to run into the top of their range. You know your big calls are "good," you're just unlucky that they had that specific hand.

A-Game Players view downswings as an opportunity to regroup and improve their game. Sometimes a bad run really can be chalked up to some negative variance, but an A-Game Player knows there is usually something that can be learned when it feels like the poker gods are conspiring against you. The *Never Lucky* program causes you to be oblivious to the warning signs in your game and to miss opportunities to learn from failure.

How it Serves

Players with this program often secretly (or subconsciously) root for bad beats or coolers, as it allows them the opportunity to get validation and sympathy from their peers. Viewing their failures as luck-driven rather than effort-driven, allows them to protect their ego when things go wrong.

Where it Starts

This program often starts when a sense of injustice is installed in the subconscious. Parents who are not successful themselves often protect their own ego by blaming their circumstances on outside forces. It's much easier to tell your children that their poor situation is because other people are just more fortunate than them, rather than taking personal responsibility.

It can also come from a general fear of success or failure, which has an infinite number of root causes. In a game where luck plays a role, it's the simplest way to protect your ego. If your failure is due to factors out of your control, then you never need to risk damaging your ego.

Perfectionist

How it Shows

A player who is running the *Perfectionist* program needs all conditions to be optimal in order to perform.

The perfect night's sleep.

The perfect breakfast.

The perfect morning routine.

The perfect pre-game warm up.

The perfect lineup.

Miss any of those and they might as well not even play today. Many players running this program also feel like they need to know "everything" before they're ready to start playing or move up in stakes. Players running this program know the importance of bringing their A-Game and will quit a session as soon as they feel they are playing their B-Game, even if that means leaving a still quite profitable game.

How it Hurts

An A-Game Player has strong routines and habits and puts in the time to work on their game. They are also creative, adaptable, and able to take calculated risks.

The *Perfectionist* program tries to remove the risk from a game that is built around chance and variance. It tries to turn poker into chess, which we all know it's not. In fact, poker is the profitable game it is *because* of the luck factor, not in spite of it.

Shooting for perfection may seem like a smart play, but you slash your opportunities to make profits by only playing when conditions meet an extremely high standard. A-Game Poker is all about bringing your best self to any situation, not bringing yourself only to the best situations. Players running this program often study excessively. By excessively, I mean missing out on profitable games, studying situations that have little relevance to the games they're playing, and needing to acquire an enormous amount of skill before they'll play at the next level.

How it Serves

The subconscious inherently prefers to avoid risk. This is the job it was created to do. Someone running the *Perfectionist* program takes this to the extreme. Sure, it would be fantastic if you could make a ton of profits from poker, taking almost no risks at all, but that isn't a realistic option.

This program tries to exert control over a situation that calls for smart risk-management instead. This program views the natural risks that come with poker as painful, rather than an opportunity to profit. By only playing when the conditions are "perfect" it tries to limit that pain as much as possible.

Where it Starts

The *Perfectionist* program typically finds its roots in a fear of failure. When you attempt to make every variable perfect, it comes from a place of wanting to make failure impossible. The *Perfectionist* does an exceptional job of running away from risk in a way that allows them to feel productive. They get to play the part of a successful poker player, without assuming any of the risk that comes with the job.

If I'm Not First, I'm Last

How It Shows

Players running the *If I'm Not First, I'm Last* program are typically quite resilient to tilting from variance situations. However, it's a different story when they make a mistake. These players hold themselves to an incredibly high standard, and the results can be devastating when they believe they performed even a small bit below those standards.

Players running this program tend to beat themselves up excessively for minor mistakes, and tend to ruminate over these mistakes for longer than most would consider reasonable. This rumination often extends well beyond the poker table, with a series of mistakes often "ruining" entire days or weeks and having a negative impact on their life out of the game.

How It Hurts

Players running this program often have unreasonable reactions to even the smallest of mistakes. These emotional reactions lead to tilt at the table, along with the inability to disconnect off the table. These players often find it difficult to connect with friends and family after they have a bad session. In turn, this prevents them from getting the full amount of recovery they need to perform at their best.

The extreme amount of pressure these players put on themselves, combined with a lack of recovery, means burnout is never far away. They also tend to underestimate their opponents, and approach the game with an air of superiority. Beating themselves up for mistakes shifts their thought processes away from curiosity and growth, to self-punishment and loathing. Rather than look at mistakes as an opportunity to grow, they treat them like a personality flaw that needs to be beaten out of them.

How It Serves

These players hold themselves to an incredibly high standard and are typically driven and determined to succeed. Many of the highest performing individuals use negative energy to propel themselves forward. This is a strategy that works very well until it doesn't and things come crashing down. That being said, running away from a negative emotion is a powerful driver, and players can get very far by doing so.

Where It Starts

Players with the *If I'm Not First, I'm Last* program often grew up in environments where the expectations were incredibly high for them. At some point they were made to feel like they weren't good enough unless they performed at an exceptionally high level.

Often, small mistakes were pointed out and punished, even when the player was doing well in most other areas of their life. Think about the parent that asks what went wrong when you got an A- in Algebra, even though you had an A+ in everything else. There are also times when players become known for being an exceptional player, and that becomes part of their identity. They receive validation from the poker community, and that fills a void they have in other areas of their life. In that case, they may feel the need to execute flawlessly or risk losing the praise and admiration of their peers.

PRO CASE STUDY

JASON KOON

HIGH-STAKES PROFESSIONAL WITH OVER $52,000,000 IN LIVE EARNINGS

I was already playing very high stakes when I started working with Elliot. In fact, I started right around the time that some of the biggest games I've ever played in started to run.

What caused me to reach out to a mindset coach was noticing that my emotional responses to the game were well below my skill set. It didn't make sense to allow such a wide gap to continue at the level I was competing at. The interesting thing was, often it wasn't even situations in the biggest game that had the most significant impact on my mindset and emotional state. At the time, I regularly experienced seven-figure swings. Occasionally, I played a Sunday session online to keep my MTT game sharp, and there were times when I'd be more upset losing a hand in a $2,000 tournament than I'd been when swinging three million the day before.

What triggered me the most was situations where I felt like I "Got got." If I felt like a player tricked or "owned" me somehow, it hurt me. This compounded when I played lower stakes, where I was "supposed" to be the best player at the table.

The worst part was that I carried that with me off the table. I would shut down my computer and go hang out with my wife, and instead of being present and enjoying a nice meal with her, all I could think about was how some guy on the internet had just beat me in a hand in a $2,600 tournament.

This wasn't a healthy way to approach the game, and it became pretty taxing to always carry these emotions with me off the table, especially when it was situations like this that had no real impact on my long-term results. The overall theme quickly became obvious when I started digging into this issue with Elliot.

Growing up my family was poor, and that led to bullying. I was ridiculed for not having nice clothes, the typical barbs you get at that age. One memory that stuck out was wearing this pair of hand-me-down Nike swimming trunks. You could tell they were second-hand because the Nike swoosh was hanging on by just a few threads. I was bullied relentlessly for this, and I remember feeling so worthless in those moments and wishing so strongly that people could see that I was worthy.

As I climbed the poker ranks, the notoriety I gained finally gave me the sense of self-worth I had always desired. Being a great player became part of my identity, and that meant my ego took a hit anytime I made a mistake or got outplayed. It felt like the poker world wouldn't admire me anymore, that I wouldn't be good enough. It wasn't a personal thing with those who outplayed me, it was more just me feeling like I should never be outplayed or I wouldn't be good enough. The worst part was that I wasn't able to be fully present with my family and friends because I was stuck caring about what people I didn't even know might think about me.

Working with Elliot, I was able to shift my source of self-worth. Rather than needing external validation to feel that I was worthy, I started to believe that my worth was inherent. This meant that I was free to play my best poker, and when I inevitably made a mistake or got outplayed, I was able to let it go and move on. I learned self-forgiveness and had fewer expectations of what I wanted the world to give me.

That's resulted in me being more present and focused when I'm spending time with the people that matter most to me, the people who care about me even if I busted every tournament I played earlier that day. When I have a losing session or play a hand poorly, I'm able to forgive myself and learn from the mistake, rather than being preoccupied with the result. The shift has been life-changing, with better results on the table and, more important, with me being able to fully enjoy that success.

Reading these examples, along with the stories from some of the game's best, should start to draw back the curtain on the subconscious programs that are keeping you from becoming an A-Game Player.

Please remember that the reason I give these programs names is to make it easier for you to recognize patterns in them that may have similarities to your own situation. However, similar does not mean identical. Whereas a computer program will be identical on all systems you download it to, your personal subconscious programs are unique to you. The shapes may be similar, but the forms are not.

This is why working with a mindset & performance coach who specializes in identifying the Detrimental Mental Programs you might be running can be so beneficial to accelerating your journey to becoming an A-Game Player.

Poker is a game that rapidly brings these programs to the surface, and my experience shows that they are the single biggest barrier to success in the game.

To learn more about working with a coach trained by me, visit the resource center for the book at: AGamePoker.com/resources

CHAPTER 31

PULLING BACK THE CURTAIN

While I'm not fully able to recreate the experience of working with a coach on your Detrimental Mental Programs, I do have an exercise that does a good job in helping you understand what's holding you back from being an A-Game Player and starts the process of uncovering the Detrimental Mental Programs that are at the root of the problem.

This is going to be an interactive exercise, so what I'd like you to do right now is to grab the document or notebook that you've been using for your A-Game Exercises. During this quick exercise I'm going to ask you to do some visualization, and you may want to find spots where you can pause and close your eyes to make the visuals more vivid. You'll get the most out of this exercise if you do it in a quiet place where you won't be distracted.Now that you're ready to jot down some quick notes, I want you to start thinking about the Fundamental Performance Question.

"What are the best in the world doing that I'm not?"

We covered all of the major points in The Anatomy of an A-Game Player, so you'll have lots of data points to work with. What are the things that you *know you* should be doing but aren't? The things that you know the A-Game Players we've discussed are doing, that for some reason you've been holding yourself back from.

Maybe it's creating a detailed schedule that covers all the foundational activities we discussed. Maybe it's sticking to a fitness plan or creating a nutritional strategy that fuels your optimal performance? Maybe it's studying the game frequently enough and in a way to actually make skill gains so that you can outpace your competition. Maybe it's simply approaching the game with the commitment and mindset of a professional athlete. And maybe there are in-game situations where you know you're not playing your best, you're playing with a lack of focus or you're tilting and making bad decisions based on emotion when you actually know the correct play.

Don't rush through this part. This book is not going anywhere, so take the time to be as detailed and thorough as possible. When you've completed the list, I want you to think about the one that stands out the most. The one that's just harder than it should be. Circle that one on your paper, highlight it, underline it, whatever you need to do to make it stand out.

Now, I want you to think about how the idea of doing this task, taking that risk, or taking that action makes you feel.

Does it make you feel anxious?

Do you feel a pressure in your chest, or a sickness in your stomach?

Does it just feel like there is an invisible forcefield holding you back from doing what you know you should be doing?

Zone into the way that it feels to you and write that sensation down. And now, as you focus in on that thought or that feeling, I'd like you to think back to other times in your life when you felt or acted in a similar way. If you want to close your eyes and visualize that feeling, go ahead. This exercise will be much more powerful if you do.

Just think about that feeling and open your eyes once you're able to fully feel it. Now, think back through the years to the different times you've had that sensation, whatever it might be. As you go through this process, you might notice there's a theme here. Those who procrastinate, have been procrastinating for a long time. The people holding themselves back from success have experienced self-sabotage or confidence issues at different parts of their life. What do you notice about your poker game that has shown up in other areas of your life over the years? You can close your eyes again, opening them as you really connect with this feeling. And now...

I want you to start to trace that feeling all the way back to its origin. And as you go through this process you'll start to bring up some memories from your past. You might find that it started when a teacher said you would never amount to anything. If there were issues within your family that made you feel a lack of confidence or that you didn't deserve to be successful or loved. Maybe someone in your family had a disdain for people with wealth, telling you that money is the root of all evil. Perhaps it stems from bullying issues at school that damaged your confidence and hampered your ability to show the world your full capabilities.

Whatever it is, start to visualize the memory...

Take a moment to write down what you remember, then close your eyes and take just a little bit longer to make the memory even more vivid in your mind's eye. Open up your eyes again when your inner vision is as clear as it can be. Now, start to look at it from the outside, as if you were looking with your adult eyes, your adult understanding in this situation. I'd like you to start reframing these memories from your past in a very different way.

I'd like you to start to see that the teacher who said you wouldn't amount to anything or mocked you in class in front of the other students was probably just having a bad day. Maybe they were stressed out, underpaid, overwhelmed or even had a fight with their spouse and they lashed out at you, not thinking anything of it.But you took it to heart, and it's been festering inside you for your entire life. Or perhaps it's bullying issues that have damaged your confidence. Looking at bullying, in most situations, there's a 10-year-old child being mean and terrible to another 10-year-old just to make themselves feel better. It might not be a nice experience, but to our child-self it seemed like the end of the world. Then there were the families who looked down on wealthier families to compensate for the disappointment they felt in themselves; it was easier to project their feelings of inadequacy onto others than confront their own shortcomings.

Start reframing these experiences and seeing them for what they really are, so you can start to release the emotions around them. The reality is that we create these programs in our childhood and teenage years, and then find ourselves repeating them throughout our lives unless we do something about it.

Now, take a deep breath.

In…and out…

Deep breath in…

…and out.

Excellent work. You've just taken your initial step in starting to unwind this particular Detrimental Mental Program, your first step in overcoming it so that you won't feel or act this way anymore. It's not who you are that prevents you from taking these actions or from becoming an A-Game Player, it's simply a program that you've learned that's not allowing you to fulfill your full potential. I'm here to help you start changing this program, to help you see that these issues are not innate personality traits. You're not anxious, you just learned to be anxious. You're not a tilter, you just learned to tilt. You're not bad at studying, you've just been afraid of what would happen if you tried and fell short. You're not afraid of success, you've learned to be afraid of success. You're not afraid to make the right decisions, you've simply learned to take the easy path because it serves the purpose of protecting your ego or keeping you safe in some way or another.

These programs have been running in the background, preventing anything else from coming in. And it is time to get past them at long last. Just being aware that these Detrimental Mental Programs exist puts you well ahead of most of your competition. What I really want you to take away from this exercise is to identify the list of items you know are holding you back, the list you just wrote out minutes ago. They aren't innate personality flaws; they're more like a weighted vest you're wearing that you can choose to discard when you decide that you really want to make serious progress on your biggest dreams and goals. When you shed the burdens you've carried around for so long, amazing things will start to happen.

Imagine waking up each morning feeling fresh, focused, and confident that you will perform your best during today's session. How well will you sleep at night if each day you go to bed knowing you made significant progress on your biggest goals and visions? Imagine if the stress, frustration, fear and internal resistance you feel now were to simply melt away, allowing the best version of yourself to come through. Understanding the true nature of your subconscious resistance is the first step in making that happen, and that's exactly what we've just accomplished together.

Now, before we conclude this exercise, I'll ask you for one more thing. Take a look at that list you just made, the list of actions you know you *should* be doing but aren't. I want you to think about a decisive action you can take *today* to remove at least one of those items from your list. I am certain there is something on the list that you can take action on the next time you set down this book. I want today to be the day you get the ball rolling.

Not tomorrow.

Not next week.

Not next month.

And definitely not next year.

You know these are all things you should be doing, that you need to be doing, if you're going to achieve the levels of success you desire in this game. You're now aware of the subconscious programs that have prevented you from taking action previously, and with the knowledge you now have, that *changes* today. Now that you're aware of the subconscious blocks in your life, everything gets easier from here. You can now naturally approach this area with more conscious awareness and feel less resistance when trying to implement the strategies and tactics outlined in this book.

Please note, while I consider this a powerful exercise, and a good introduction to what it's like to work with one of my trained mindset & performance coaches, it's only possible to touch on a fraction of what it's like to do this work directly.

While this exercise is designed to get the ball rolling, it is incredibly difficult to dissolve these programs on your own.

To learn more about working with my team of coaches, you can find additional information in the resource page for this book at <u>AGamePoker.com/resources</u>.

PRO CASE STUDY

MATT BERKEY

HIGH-STAKES CASH GAME PROFESSIONAL & FOUNDER OF SOLVE FOR WHY

When I reached out to Elliot, I was two years into playing 300/600/1200 three days a week. The first year and a half went well. I might have run a bit under expectation, but I won. Things took a turn, however, and I was on a six-month downswing where I'd lost 22 out of 26 sessions, which added up to a $5,000,000 downswing. It was 25 or 30x, my biggest downswing ever, and it was abundantly clear that it was more rooted in my mental game than mechanics.

Through poker I had gone from being extremely broke to having a relatively significant net worth, certainly more than I had ever experienced before. As I got into the big game and started winning, I quickly became a millionaire. Growing up in poverty and chaos had left me with a resistance to affluence that showed itself around the million-dollar mark. Calling myself a millionaire and attaining that level of wealth, there was a disconnect between my subconscious identity and the achievements I was making in my life. Every time I crossed the million-dollar threshold, it would trigger something in me and I would very quickly have a downswing. Only this time, it was quite extended and was cutting into my net worth significantly.

I've never been one to lean on people in my life for support, whether it be friends and family or a mentor or coach. Being a problem solver was part of my identity, and I always had the sense that I had to work through things on my own.

However, when someone recommended that I connect with Elliot, things were bad enough that I was willing to try anything. We quickly developed a strong rapport. Elliot spoke to me in a language that made me feel like I was understood, like he knew where I was coming from in this self-isolated/self-diagnosed high-performing problem-solver mentality. I let my guard down and allowed him to do what he does best and walk me through the areas that could potentially lead my subconscious into these self-destructive patterns. The resolution was coming to grips with the fact that variance exists in everyone's life, and it's better to live up to or beyond your expectations than to be the type of person full of potential who never actually executes.

Something that sticks out is the example of the kid who got by in high school without ever having to study and was happy to get a B+ instead of putting in ten percent more effort to get an A. That was me to a T. From working with Elliot, I understood that if you do the same thing in poker, you will feel very cheated because variance is already a leveler. When you add the lack of effort necessary to overcome said variance and achieve significant results in this game, the equation just falls short. There's no room in this game to shoot yourself in the foot, and that finally became clear to me.

The funny part is that I started getting invited to better games because of the $5,000,000 downswing. I could play twice as often and begin to put in actual volume at these stakes. It was a massive opportunity that came from a bad time, and because of the work we put in on my mindset, I could take full advantage of it. I won 27 out of 30 sessions, ultimately culminating in the work we did around the 2016 Super High Roller Bowl, which was far and away the biggest tournament I had ever played. I got fifth place in that for $1,100,000, which got me even on the 5 million downswing.

The big picture takeaway for me is how important it is not to ignore the mental side of the game and not wait until you hit rock bottom to work on this area of your game. It's easy for us, as professionals who spend all of our time crunching numbers and analyzing data, to believe it's just as simple as showing up, executing, and putting in volume. The actual act of showing up, executing, and putting in volume is heavily rooted in how emotionally stable and mentally tenacious you are. Your resiliency and the ability to dust yourself off and do this repeatedly is essential. You almost have to be a little bit of a crazy person or be incredibly dialed into your mental game to do that consistently.

The best players in the world don't wait until the technical game has passed them by to start studying and improving their game. They understand that constant growth is essential to maintain and increase their edge over time. While I'm thankful that I could dig myself out of such a massive hole, it's clear that the GTO move would have been to invest in my mindset when things were going well. In today's game, you must take advantage of every possible edge. So much opportunity is lost by getting yourself into a negative spiral and waiting until the last moment to get help in an area that all serious professionals should be doing anyway.

CHAPTER 32

DEALING WITH DOWNSWINGS

I imagine if I surveyed everyone who was about to start this book, dealing with downswings would be one of the top answers to the question, "What's holding you back?"

Downswings are the true test of your A-Game Player status. The swings of the game will test the resolve of even the mentally strongest players out there. The truth is, most players fail this test. The inability to deal with an extended losing streak is what ends the majority of poker careers. If you play this game for long enough you're going to be confronted by a downswing bigger and crazier than anything you thought was possible. When this time comes. you have two options:

The first is to curse your bad luck, constantly think about how bad you run, and allow negative thought patterns to creep into your game, harming both your ability to focus, and make your best decisions in-game.

The second is to stay accountable and strong, examine your game for weaknesses and creeping bias, and to continue playing A-Game Poker session after session.

Everyone wants to choose the second option, but it's only A-Game Players who are actually able to take that path. Now, it's pretty easy to see how an extended losing streak can lead to some mental lapses at the table. If not properly dealt with, the emotions accumulate until tiny triggers that wouldn't have bothered you in the past, now put you on full-blown tilt.

What's less obvious is how a losing streak can affect the technical side of your game. If, over the last few weeks, you've been running into the top of your opponent's range, you might subconsciously start to shift the range you give your opponents, leading to a drop in your win rate. So, while you might not be smashing monitors, this is actually even more dangerous, as it's not as obvious a problem as the extreme emotions.

Now, when you first started this book, chances are one of the areas of change you were looking for was an increased ability to deal with downswings. The truth is, I almost didn't include this chapter in this book. When you apply the concepts you've learned so far, and go all-in on with the systems that are still to come, the impact that downswings have on your game are greatly diminished. There is no magic bullet when it comes to the ability to deal with downswings. What matters is your system, your process, and your approach to the game. This is what you trust when it feels like you can do nothing right. The A-Game Poker System is the lighthouse that safely guides you back to shore in even the roughest of waters. So yes, I could have left this chapter out and you would have had pretty much all the tools needed to deal with the worst downswings the game can throw at you. Everything you've discovered in this book so far is exactly what you need to lean on when the game puts you to the test.

With that being said, I have a powerful framework for putting the final nail in the coffin of the downswings that are impacting your game and enable you to play your best in all circumstances. The words that we use, both internally and externally have a massive impact on our mindset, in fact in many ways they *are* the manifestation of our mindset. Now, I want you to consider how you talk about downswings and how you hear those around you talk about them. Set the book down, think about it and then come back to me. Did you do it? Great.

In my private client work I've noticed a very distinct pattern in how poker players talk about downswings and, in turn, how they think about them. I'll often hear things like:

"I'm in the worst downswing of my life."

or

"Elliot, can you please help me get through this downswing?"

and

"I just need to ride out this downswing and then things will be better on the other side."

Now what do you notice about these statements? If it's nothing, that's okay. These are incredibly common statements in the poker community, so very few will notice anything wrong with them, especially if they are not A-Game Players. In all of the above statements, the person speaking them used language that was assuming they are in the middle of a downswing. And what's the problem with that? Well, the truth is, there is no such thing as being in the middle of a downswing. In reality, a downswing is only a pattern of worse than expected results that you view in the past. Yet the majority of poker players, including many professionals, extrapolate these past events into future events. So, here's the truth about downswings:

There is no such thing as being *in* a downswing.

Each hand you play is an independent event, and outside of the information you gather on your opponents and the information they gather on you, what happens in previous hands has no connection with what happens in future hands. That is, unless you allow it to.

Let's look at two different ways to frame a downswing. First, is the typical:

"I'm in a downswing and need to ride it out."

The other is:

"Over the last month I've experienced worse than expected outcomes."

What might seem like a tiny change of perspective, can make all the difference. When you look at a losing streak as simply something that happened in the past, and understand that it only impacts you in the future if you allow it to, then you can continue to play A-Game Poker each session. If you believe that you're in the middle of a downswing, it's almost impossible to not change your game as a reaction to this belief.

Just think of the phrase *riding out a downswing*. What imagery does this conjure up? What comes to mind when I hear that, is that you're in the middle of a big storm and need to board up your windows, seek cover, and wait out the storm. If you have this mindset, how do you think it might affect your game? Chances are it will be significant, even if the semantic difference is subtle. Maybe you start to take fewer opportunities to bluff, even if it's a good spot. Maybe you start to flat hands or just call bets when the correct play would be to three-bet or check-raise. And maybe you start giving your opponents more credit for big hands than they deserve, making big folds that you shouldn't. All of this because of one simple shift in wording and mindset. If you believe that a downswing is something you can be in at the present, then your mind is going to react to that belief in ways that are not beneficial to playing A-Game Poker. This is the classic definition of trying to control the uncontrollable. This is how a streak of worse than expected results can creep into your game and take what is normal poker variance and have it spiral out of control, not due to bad luck but due to poor play.

So, the key to dealing with downswings is to understand their true nature. A downswing is simply a pattern of past events that you notice in the present moment; it's not something you can predictively be *in,* either now or in the future. When you hold this frame, then downswings lose all the mystical power that we tend to give them, and you can go on just playing poker. Now, obviously that's easier said than done, so I'm going to give you four mindset shifts that should help with the process.

Each Hand Is a New Puzzle

We've talked about this mindset multiple times, and it's important enough to recap it here. To embrace this mindset is to embrace A-Game Poker. It's not about what happened last hand, 30 minutes ago, last week, last month, or last year. When you play poker all you have is the hand in front of you. It's your job to use all the information available to you, and the full extent of your poker skills, to make the best decision you can possibly make in the moment. Yes, information you gather from hand to hand has an impact on future decisions, but the results do not.

Just because you had a 100 bb stack the hand before, doesn't mean you need to try to get it back if you lost a big pot and now have 20 bb. Every hand is a new puzzle, and it's the job of the A-Game Player to play that one hand as best you can. This is a simple mantra, but fully embracing it is one of the biggest mindset shifts you can possibly make.

Assuming It's Your Fault

The next mindset shift for dealing with downswings is to assume it's your fault. If you have an extended losing streak, rather than assuming that it's just bad luck, dig into your game and assume that there is something you're doing wrong that is causing the losses. The truth is, everyone has a massive amount of room for growth, even those who are at top of the game. So, even if you truly are going through a streak of negative variance, it doesn't hurt to dig deep into your game.

Every time I've had a client go through a really horrendous downswing, when they stopped to assess and dig into their game, or had help from someone else to do so, they were able to find a significant flaw, which, when addressed, helped turn things around. So, rather than blame variance, look for ways you can improve your game and turn variance into less of a factor.

I'm not telling you to randomly change your strategy when going through a downswing. I'm saying that you should take a hard and honest look at what you're doing that might be contributing, but not make major changes without evidence. This mindset shift is all about understanding how the quality of your decisions determines the quality of your results. If you aren't getting the results you want, it's incumbent upon you to explore the quality of your decisions, but it's not a quality decision to make major changes just because the results haven't worked out in your favor recently.

Choose a Different Window

The third mindset shift is to choose a different window. Just as a downswing cannot exist in the present or the future, it can also only live in the window of time that we frame around it. Maybe you've lost three sessions in a row, but if you look at your last 10 sessions, you're highly profitable. In that case, what's the point of looking at the last three sessions? And what's the point in looking at 10 sessions when you can look at the last six months? Something that I suggest my clients do when they're feeling stressed from an extended losing streak is to adjust the window of time they're looking at.

Did you have a bad month?

What do your results for the last three months look like?

What about over the last year?

Poker is a game that has no end, and the windows of time that we group our results in are usually arbitrary and pointless. If you notice yourself struggling when looking at short-term results, just choose a different window to look at. If you don't like the results that this new window shows, well, then maybe it's time to take a look at your overall game and see what the problem is. Results over a short time frame only have meaning if we give them meaning, and now that you understand the truth about downswings and are approaching each hand as a new puzzle, you have the ability to remove the meaning you might have put on them in the past.

Lean on the A-Game Poker System

The final mindset shift for dealing with downswings is to lean into the A-Game Poker System. With this system you have all the tools you need to continue playing A-Game Poker, no matter what the game throws at you. If you find that a downswing is taking you out of your A-Game mindset, take a look at how you're applying the system, come back and revisit parts of this book (chances are you'll pick up something new or notice something you missed), and if that doesn't feel like it's quite enough to jog you out of a rut, consider investing further in yourself with my A-Game Poker Masterclass.

PRO CASE STUDY

ALEX FOXEN

HIGH-STAKES MTT PROFESSIONAL WITH OVER $30,000,000 IN LIVE EARNINGS

At the start of 2022, everything was clicking on all cylinders with my game. I won't say that I believed I had solved everything, but I was close, especially regarding the mental side of the game. Typically, I can handle the negative side of the game well, but I've run into trouble with accumulated feelings and downswings that seem to go on and on. The longer it lasts, the more it builds, to the point where situations that are typically easy to deal with get blown way out of proportion. Negative thoughts creep in, like:

"If I've been on a downswing this long, what's stopping it from lasting another whole year?"

Once I get into that cycle of negativity, my focus shifts from the process of my play to the bad luck I'm experiencing, ruminating about everything that could go wrong. I almost fall into a gambling mentality at that point. Rather than focusing on how I'm playing each hand, I see each entry as a lotto ticket, just praying that this will be the one to turn things around.

I hit up Elliot just before the WSOP in 2022, when I was at one of the lowest points in my career in terms of my mindset. Approaching the WSOP as a gambler is a recipe for disaster, and I needed to make sure everything was on point so I could take back control of my results rather than simply hope things would get better.

There were two problems that Elliot and I worked through that turned things around. Elliot discovered that I was running a program of entitlement, and we got to the root of the problem with a memory from when I was six or seven years old. My little sister had a ball that she was playing with, and as little kids do, she got distracted and went to play with something else on the other side of the room. I started playing with the ball, and my mom came in. As she did, my sister started crying, saying I had taken the ball away from her, which I hadn't. I got sent to my room, and that feeling of unfairness stuck with me and shaped how I reacted to outcomes outside my control, first in sports with referees and coaches, then in poker with bad beats and downswings.

What really made a shift and changed the trajectory of my 2022 downswing was connecting my current situation back with a downswing I went through early in my career. Most great poker players jump-start their careers with a crazy upswing in the early days, and way more potentially great players have their careers come to an end, going through the opposite. While fighting to make it in the game, I went through a downswing that nearly took me out for *good. That really stuck with me, because Elliot and I discovered that I was still holding on to those emotions and reacting in the present day as if I were in the same situation as I was back then. The truth was, I'd had enough success to be insulated from any realistic downswing, and if I kept playing winning poker, I'd always be okay. Once I realized that and let go of the emotions I'd stowed away from that early downswing, I could start refocusing on what got me there in the first place, which was trusting my process and playing each hand like a new puzzle.*

Playing the $250k at that WSOP, I was able to register and feel excited for it, rather than having a cloud of fear and doubt over my head. Instead, I approached it like it was my Super Bowl. I was focused on my performance, doing my best, and not worrying about what would happen if I didn't win. I was able to feel confident in my decisions, able to tell myself:

"I'm going to solve a new puzzle today, and I'm going to do it better than anyone else at the table."

It was invigorating to get back to that type of mindset, and it made playing poker not only more effective but significantly more fun. Of course, it's even more fun when you get the win, and I was fortunate enough to take that one down for just over 4.5 million. Elliot helped me overcome barriers to success in my subconscious that I wasn't even aware existed. Not only was I able to work through that downswing, but being able to reframe adverse outcomes and let go of perceived injustices has allowed me to focus on what's really important and tap into the best version of myself.

CHAPTER 33

LACK OF MOTIVATION

Ever wake up feeling completely unmotivated to play? Like the last thing you want to do is get out of bed and grind out a session? After a rough couple of weeks of poker, do you start to question why you even play this crazy game at all?

As we explore some of the biggest barriers holding you back from becoming an A-Game Player, lack of motivation is a subject we must not brush over. Motivation is one of the most misunderstood topics in the world of high performance. When you become the master of your motivation and tap into it at the deepest levels, the difficult study sessions, long grinds, and A-Game work are still difficult, but you're able to accomplish them with less resistance. In fact, they seem to happen almost automatically. Bad beats roll off your back, rather than lose confidence during a downswing, you'll double down on your efforts and come out the other side better than ever.

When motivation is missing, you won't bother to study, your sessions become shorter and shorter to the point of almost disappearing entirely, and the topics we cover in this book will be barely given any thought. Poker will push you over and kick you in the teeth when you're down. Even the greatest players in the world struggle with motivation at certain points in their career. Nearly every elite poker player I've worked with has encountered at least one crisis of motivation. The ones who fail to master it are the ones whom the game passes by, who become nothing more than a flash in the pan.

In most professions if you don't wake up and go to work, you get fired. In poker, if you don't show up to work, someone else takes your spot and makes the money, but you are not missed. In fact, if you're a good player your peers are fist pumping when you don't show up. At the end of the day, you answer only to yourself. That means the bulk of your motivation must be created internally. Not sure how to do that?

First, we need to talk about what motivation is, and what it is *not*. Most poker players think being motivated means jumping out of bed in the morning, getting in the games and attacking the game with the heart of a lion, ready to crush. The problem comes when we don't feel this way and feel guilty because of it. Want to know a secret? That feeling isn't actually motivation.

When people talk about *motivation*, the term *passion* is quick to follow. You always hear people say:

"If you want to stay motivated, you just need to find and follow your passion!"

For a long time, I considered this to be rubbish advice, and I still do in terms of how most people describe and try to implement it. If you look at one of the many dictionary definitions of passion, you find this:

An intense desire or enthusiasm for something.

Passion is often viewed as a hot-burning fire you feel inside that compels you to take action. Now, don't get me wrong, this feeling that many describe as passion can be quite powerful. It does an amazing job of starting you on a path and pushing you through the initial hurdles.

There's just one problem…

The feeling described here, well that feeling *always burns* out. This is a universal truth for any undertaking in life. You start something, feel tons of so-called passion, which makes everything seem easy and wonderful at first, but then it runs out. You might think there are people out there who have this intense desire one hundred percent of the time, but they're just putting on an act in public, not showing you the hard times they encounter.

Social media has amplified this infinitely in the last decade, as people can choose to show you only the best versions of themselves. You might look at content creators, celebrities, athletes, and big-name poker players and think they're full of this energy 24/7. That's just not the reality. This is a huge problem because it gives off the impression that the only way to be successful is to always be filled with energy and excitement.

Now, why do I refer to this as "so-called passion"? Well, that's because what most people consider passion is actually something quite different. When you look back at the origins of the word *passion*, you can see that its usage has changed significantly from the way it was once used to the definition I gave a few moments ago. The word *passion* has its roots in the Latin word *patior* which means to suffer. So, the original usage of the word wasn't about a heated desire or excitement but about the willingness to suffer, to endure some pain for something that you deeply cared about. The practical differences between these two definitions couldn't be further apart, which is why so many people fail when they try to follow the advice: "Just follow your passion."

When most people hear this, they believe they need to find something where they wake up each day with an intense desire and excitement to take action. And maybe they even find this feeling, but as I mentioned earlier, that feeling ALWAYS burns out. And that can be quite confusing. Chances are that's how you felt when you first started playing poker, and you probably feel that way quite often still, but rather than always being there it likely comes and goes in waves. Chances are these are the times when you feel a lack of motivation. The problem comes when you beat yourself up over losing this feeling. You think you've lost your passion when that might not be the case at all.

To clear this up I'm going to separate the term *passion*, which is part of the root of true motivation, from this other feeling, which I will label as *infatuation*. When you look up *infatuation* in the dictionary, here is what you find:

An intense but short-lived passion or admiration for someone or something.

With that definition we are starting to differentiate the slow burning, enduring nature of true passion, from the short-lived, intense desire and excitement that is infatuation. Now, let's take a moment to discuss this pattern of infatuation when it comes to new habits or routines that you've tried to establish and failed.

The classic example of a failed routine involves going to the gym. When you first sign up for a gym or begin a new exercise routine, it's easy. You go regularly and enthusiastically. You're infatuated and energetic. It feels great to go and your body feels better. Then, a few weeks in, you hit a wall. You start saying, "Oh, maybe today, I'll just not go." Or "I don't quite have the time." Then the next day, "Oh, well, I'm still sore from my last workout, I'll just go next time."

This is the point where infatuation has burned out and the excitement has worn off. You've lost the drive to continue and you stop going all together. Infatuation was a great way to get you started, but it is not motivation, and it will not sustain. Most people don't know the difference and try to build success around infatuation, but that is like building a house on a foundation of sand.

Another great example is a romantic relationship. You meet someone special and instantly feel an intense attraction. You spend the majority of your time with them and it feels effortless. The relationship doesn't feel like work. It's easy, fun, and exciting. Then maybe six months in you notice a change. You still care for that person, but something is different. The red-hot infatuation period has passed, and you're starting to notice the flaws in the other person. The relationship now takes effort. You can no longer just float through. This is where most relationships fail, but it's also where the best relationships transform into something much stronger and more enduring. If a relationship needs that intense desire to survive, then it's doomed to fail.

The same is true for any major undertaking in life, and certainly true for poker. In fact, nothing kills infatuation as quickly as an extended losing streak in poker. You could substitute the word "relationship" for "poker" in that story and it would describe the journey all A-Game players go through.

This journey is something that I call "The Progress Path," and it describes the emotional cycle that occurs when you're developing your poker game or trying to obtain mastery in any area of life. Here's a breakdown of what the path looks like:

Initial Infatuation,

Into The Rabbit Hole,

The Grind,

The Choice,

Embrace the Grind.

The first stage is the Initial Infatuation. This is that honeymoon period we've been talking about so far. You discover the game, fall in love, and want to eat, sleep, and dream poker. Once you start to learn what it actually takes to be successful you enter the "Into the Rabbit Hole" stage. This is when you realize just how much you don't know about the game, and how much work it's going to take to get you where you want to be.Most people drop off here and just continue to play recreationally.

The next phase is what I call "The Grind," and it's the make or break time for poker players. This is where your infatuation has burned out and you've realized the full enormity of the task ahead. This is where true passion and motivation must kick in if you're going to continue on a path to success. Once you hit "The Grind," you have "The Choice," a fork in the road.

You can either choose to accept "The Grind" and move forward, quit the game completely, or continue to play the game in misery, with little or no success. There's a strong chance this is exactly where you were when you decided to pick up this book. And the goal of this book, and my A-Game Poker Masterclass, is to give you the tools to choose the correct path for you.

The final stage is to "Embrace the Grind." This is where you take the next step from simply accepting "The Grind" to fully embracing it and enjoying the deep puzzles that must be solved to move ahead. This is where the A-Game Player makes their home. They understand that success is a bumpy road with many peaks and valleys, rather than simply a straight line to the top. They know that most of the answers won't come easy, and embrace and enjoy the struggle. They have a vision for their game and life, which fuels the passion needed to accept the discomfort that can accompany growth. They embrace the challenge for as long as necessary, until the cycle repeats, and they're hit with a wave of Initial Infatuation again.

You see, this Progress Path isn't something that happens one time in a poker career. It keeps repeating again and again as your knowledge of the game grows and as you face the hard times that the game throws at you.

So, what exactly is The Grind, and how can you become someone who has the ability to embrace it? The Grind is something all poker players go through in their poker career; many times, in fact, if you play long enough. It's the point where Initial Infatuation has burned out, either through time or at the hands of some brutal variance. It's when you realize just how little you know about the game but aren't clear on how to take the next step. It's when not only do you question your game, you start to question why you play at all. Maybe sessions have lost their fun or you're too overwhelmed to study because you don't know what you need to be working on, or both.

If you've known a player (or have done this yourself) who jumps from format to format when things get tough, it's because they don't know how to get past "The Grind." By moving to a different format, they get to restart at "Initial Infatuation," which feels really good, at least for a little while. The problem with that strategy is that scant progress is made in their game as they keep jumping from format to format, just before they are able to have a big breakthrough.

Now, The Grind may sound pretty awful, but I'm going to let you in on a secret. The Grind is actually your best friend. In the moment it might feel like your worst enemy, but for those who can push through it's an amazing gift. The first reason The Grind is your best friend is because it serves as a gatekeeper for people moving along in their poker career. There are a *lot* of people who start off extremely infatuated with poker, but very few of them ever even make it to a break-even level of skill. This is because they hit The Grind and choose to not move forward. They either get frustrated and leave the game or continue to play at their current level, never making progress. The second reason that The Grind is your best friend is that it signals that you're close to a breakthrough in your game, and if you can find a way through, you'll be able to start the whole process again, just at a higher level.

So, that leads us to the question:

How *do* we Embrace the Grind?

Imagine that your poker career is a journey along a path. When you hit The Grind it's like a fork in the road. One path continues along the same road you were on, it looks easy enough, but descends into a dark forest further down the road. The other path goes up into nicer looking terrain, there's just one problem. There's a chasm between where you are now and the other side. You know it's the better path, but to get across you're going to need a bridge. Metaphorically speaking, the bridge to cross that chasm is motivation. To get across to that higher path you're going to need some tools. Before we can talk about how to master your motivation, we first need to define what it actually means, Here's the definition of motivation:

The reason or reasons one has for acting or behaving in a particular way.

That's interesting, isn't it? Because you probably think about motivation as a force, as a pair of hands placed right behind your shoulder blades pushing you forward relentlessly. But motivation isn't a force, it's the answer to a series of "Why's."

Why am I doing this?

Why do I want to do this?

Why should I do this?

Why am I willing to endure some hardship?

Every decision you make starts with a why. And you had better have a good answer ready. Because when you don't have a strong answer, or you have no answer at all, you're going to naturally seek out and take the path of least resistance instead of the path that pushes you through The Grind and on to bigger and better things. Without a strong reason why, you lead a life of randomness and condemn yourself to short-term thinking and short-term pleasure seeking.

The search for your deep motivation starts with your Vision. Namely, how do you picture your life unfolding in the long run? Where do you want to go? Who do you want to be? And what do you want to accomplish? When you don't have a clear picture in your mind of the shape you want your life to take long-term, you get stuck in the short-term. When you face any resistance along the way, you get easily distracted and dissuaded, and you choose the easy path. Rather than play the volume you know you should, work on your game, or focus on your health, you throw on a marathon session of your favorite TV show or fire up some video games because it makes you feel good right now, and you have no motivation to build the bridge and push past The Grind.

This is why I started the "Becoming An A-Game Player" section with a simple vision exercise, and dedicate an entire module to vision-crafting in my A-Game Poker Masterclass. Taking the time to figure out who you want to become and what you want to be doing, gives you a push to become an A-Game Player. Here's something to remember:

Your long-term vision dictates your short-term decisions, and your short-term decisions dictate your long-term success.

If you have a strong vision, you won't find pleasure in the short-term distractions that take you away from your vision. When you start to go off track, you'll feel an internal conflict.

A conflict created by the fact that you're going against your vision, and that conflict is your motivation. You'll say to yourself:

"I'm in The Grind. This is hard, but doing what I need to do to move forward is going to lead me toward my life's vision. It's difficult but the benefit in the future outweighs the cost now."

Whether you're trying to save money, get in shape, push through a hard study session, or grind through a period where nothing goes your way, your vision—your why—is the lynchpin to your motivation. Think about it like this:

Every time you walk into a grocery store, you don't have to consciously remind yourself not to steal. You don't have to say to yourself, "Okay, I'm *not* going to steal from the store today." Why is that? It's because you have a strong vision of yourself as someone who doesn't steal, likely thanks to the way you were raised. Your parents probably taught you to respect the property of others and to be a good citizen. Therefore, stealing isn't a part of the person you are today. It isn't a part of your mental or physical fabric; it's not part of your identity. Stealing doesn't fit the vision you've created for yourself, which is why you don't have to use willpower to keep yourself from stealing every time you walk into a grocery store.

When you have a strong vision of yourself, willpower is no longer necessary because the perceived right actions are those that align with your vision. With a vision, you're aligning the actions of today with your future self. Sure, you may want everything in the grocery store for free, but you have a vision of yourself as an honest person who doesn't steal.

That is the power of vision. Once you build a strong vision, you give yourself an identity that will naturally drive you in the direction you want to go. At every opportunity over the course of this book I have driven home the point that A-Game Players are different. They see the game of poker and the game of life through a different lens. They take uncommon actions so that they can get uncommon results. You have dedicated your time, energy, effort and focus into this book, and it's time for you to fully embrace the identity of an A-Game Player. This is not a title that I can bestow upon you, this is something that you must choose to become yourself. If you see yourself as a highly successful professional poker player, then let that story guide you and take action as if you are that player now. Remember, your long-term vision dictates your short-term decisions, and your short-term decisions dictate your long-term success.

If you want something in life, then you need to be the type of person who achieves that result. If you want to be fit and healthy then that must be part of your vision and you must be a fit and healthy person. If you want great results in poker, then you must approach the game as a successful player would. Your results are the by-product of the type of person you become.

In this section, we've answered the question: "What's Holding You Back?"

Detrimental Mental Programs,

Dealing with downswings,

And lack of motivation.

You have a framework for what the best players in the world are doing that you're not, you've learned and actively implemented the foundational strategies of my A-Game Poker system, and we've started the process of clearing away all the excuses that are blocking you from getting there. It's been quite the journey, and if you've implemented even a small segment of what we've covered, I imagine you are already noticing a significant shift in the trajectory of your life and game. The final question we have to answer is, what comes next?

YOUR NEXT STEP

I am a collector of stories.

This book started with Phil Galfond's observation about me that there is little I'd rather be doing than helping others unlock their best version of themselves. This is true, and stories of success are the positive reinforcement that fuels me to continue to improve as a coach and create content such as this book. When I hear about a client winning a WSOP bracelet, having their biggest month at cash games, winning an Olympic medal or UFC championship, selling their company for a massive multiple...it fuels me.As do stories of players changing the trajectory of their life with my A-Game Poker Masterclass, or seeing positive reviews of the Primed Mind app, or, if I earned it, 5-star reviews of this book. It all fuels me.

By reading this book and completing the exercises within, my hope is that you have gained the conviction that you are the author of your own story, and it's a story I'm excited to one day hear from you, myself. If you choose to continue down the A-Game path, your story is one you'll be writing for the rest of your life. This book is just the beginning.

Remember:

Happily Ever After does not exist.

That means no matter where you're at in your story, happiness and fulfillment are available along the way. Whatever your vision may be, you now have the tools to shift it from dream to reality. If you're determined to continue on this journey, you don't have to do it alone. I've created a suite of tools designed to help you move forward, no matter what chapter you may be on. I'll outline a few of them here, and you can learn more about them (as well as claim discounts on many of the tools) in the resource center for this book: **AGamePoker.com/resources**

Primed Mind

Primed Mind originated as a collaboration between myself and Fedor Holz. Fedor received so much value from our work together that he wanted to find a way to make my mindset coaching strategies widely available.

The app uses audios called Primers to generate the exact mindset you need to in that moment.

In addition to working with me directly, many of my most successful clients use Primed Mind regularly to stay on track and consistently execute at a high level.

In addition to an entire section dedicated to poker, there are Primers designed for nearly any situation imaginable. From getting in the zone, injecting confidence and motivation, to getting your best night's sleep, Primed Mind gives you the ability to take control of your mindset in just minutes a day.

The A-Game Poker Masterclass

If you found this book valuable and want to continue on your journey to becoming an A-Game Player, then enrolling in my A-Game Poker Masterclass is the logical next step.

This six-module video course reinforces all of the topics in this book, expanding on many of the topics as well as introducing some more advanced A-Game Poker strategies. By now you should know how much I value active over passive learning methods. That's why I designed this to be much more than a typical online course. Rather, this is an interactive training program. Each module has its own workbook for you to fill out as you work your way through the content.

The A-Game Poker Masterclass is all about taking action and making real, meaningful, change in your game and life. The workbook and exercises have been designed to get you specific outcomes that move you along the path to A-Game Poker.

PRO CASE STUDY

LARA EISENBERG

WORLD SERIES OF POKER BRACELET WINNER

I imagine most of the stories you'll hear in this book are from professional players. Knowing the clients Elliot works with, I'm confident they'll be from some of the best players in the world. That's exciting, and I can't wait to read them myself, yet my story is a bit different.

Poker has always been a recreational activity for me. As a full-time physician, I can allocate much less time to the game than a full-time pro. But just because I'm a recreational player doesn't mean I treat the game like a hobby. I would wager that I approach the game more professionally than many pros do, and I owe that mindset to what I've learned from Elliot.

I started in poker during the Moneymaker days, dabbling online and then going to Atlantic City on the weekends. As I became more serious about learning, I picked up some courses and eventually stumbled upon Elliot's website when he was selling individual warm-

up and cool-down MP3s. They were great for my game, and I felt so much better being able to get in the zone quickly and then disconnect equally as fast once the tournament was over.

I was among the first to sign up when Elliot offered a Pilot Program for his A-Game Poker Masterclass. The course is incredible. It covers so many topics in-depth, from preparation to performance, managing breaks, and everything from exercise, nutrition, recovery, and other lifestyle factors that make someone an "A-Game Player."

Having it all in one concise system makes it easy to remember and implement. Also, using the companion journal helps reinforce and put what I was learning into practice.

It's so much more than "Hey, don't go on tilt and have a positive attitude." It's a blueprint for creating an effective poker player and using the game to build your desired life. The best part is that a strong mental game can give me an edge against my peers and narrow the gap between myself and the more experienced professional players.

Pros have so much more time to invest into studying the game, and it is surprising that many don't prioritize putting in the work to ensure they can apply those skills at the tables. As long as I play part-time, I can't control that time gap, so I have to make it up in other ways. Those areas are mindset, efficient study, exercise, diet, sleep, and everything the A-Game Poker Masterclass encapsulates. Many pros still underestimate these areas, and it's why I've succeeded, even with the limitations in place.

Since going through the course, I've won a WSOP circuit ring, my first WSOP bracelet and got 2nd in the WPT Prime Championship for $481,000. Those big scores and the consistent profits I've made have been very validating. I'm proud of my accomplishments, and my confidence has grown significantly. With *everything I've learned from the Elliot and the A-Game Poker Masterclass, I'm excited to see what's possible as I shift more of my time and attention to poker.*

Private Mindset & Performance Coaching

No matter how much you learn about mindset and performance, none of it is relevant if you have Detrimental Mental Programs blocking you from taking action. This is the missing link for most personal development systems.

The backbone of my mindset & performance coaching methodology is quickly identifying the biggest Detrimental Mental Programs holding you back, and rapidly eliminating them, allowing you to easily take the actions needed to become the best version of yourself.

While working with me directly won't make financial sense for anyone playing outside of the biggest games, I've trained a team of coaches in my methodology for eliminating Detrimental Mental Programs; they're experts in my A-Game Poker System and have a deep understanding of what it takes to succeed in modern poker games. While there are other practitioners who know how to work with subconscious programs, and mindset coaches who focus on poker, my team are world class at both.

Obviously, I'm biased, but after seeing the results of my clients, as well as results of clients who have worked with other members of my team, it's my opinion that any poker player looking to be a long-term winning player should work regularly with a mindset & performance coach from our team.

Compared to the strategic side of the game, there are still so many exploitable edges to be found in the mindset/A-Game poker realm. Not doing so is akin to being offered private access to GTO solutions in the early days of solvers, but turning them down because you want to do it all yourself.

In this book you've heard stories from players who have worked with me directly, and by working with my team of coaches you can experience a similar level of coaching no matter where you are in your A-Game Poker journey. The journey to A-Game Poker means a commitment to excellence, and it's a journey you don't need to take alone. The tools mentioned above are designed to press the fast-forward button on that journey so that you can reach new heights at a pace much faster than you ever could on your own.

If you haven't already, head over to the resource section at <u>AGamePoker.com/resources</u> to learn more.

If You Forget Everything Else, Remember This

Your greatest gift to the world is becoming the best version of yourself. Many of my clients worry that a life dedicated to poker doesn't do enough to contribute to the betterment of society. It's not my place to answer that question for them one way or the other, but my experience has shown me that while we have significant agency in the outcome of our lives, there are certain innate drivers and motivators that inform the areas into which we're able to put our full focus.

Human potential is a magnificent thing, and it's my firm belief that we are only scraping the surface of what we're truly capable of. If poker is what calls to you, then showing the world what you're capable of in the game can not only allow you to live a fulfilled life, but also inspire others to be the best version of themselves.

Millions of people find inspiration daily in the physical feats of professional athletes, the innovation of visionary entrepreneurs, and in those who demonstrate mastery over their craft. Excellence itself is inspirational, so if you're able to achieve your biggest goals and live your best life, it will be impossible not to make positive waves along the way.

Throughout this book I've mentioned that A-Game Players are different, and I hope that by completing this book you are feeling that shift, whether it's a tiny change for the better, or a massive transformation. Thank you for having me along for your journey, and for allowing me to be part of your story. I know you're capable of greatness, so go out there and crush it, and when you do please make sure to send me your story.

Acknowledgments

It's time to thank the people who made this book happen, firstly my wife Ali who supported me through a career change and allowed me to follow the dream of helping high performers improve their mindsets. Thirteen years ago, the world was a different place and coaching was anything but mainstream, but her faith in me and my plan is the reason my career and any of this exists.

My twins Launa and Winter for bringing me joy everyday. My parents Bernard, Sue and Paul, and my brother Matt, thank you for the love and support over the years.

Ryan Carter, my business partner, and the man who's helped me develop and translate my concepts and teachings into this book, along with the multiple courses we've built together. Thanks for your trust in me, and all the effort over the years. Adrienne Carter, you've become an amazing coach and your effort has guided the company and helped our success.

My introduction to the poker world was by random chance: Francine thank you for introducing me to what could be possible in poker. Jonathan Little, Lauren Kling, Gabrielle Kollander, Daniel Dvoress and YourDoomPoker, for being some of the early adopters who were happy to share my name with the media. Without those willing to be first to the business could never have been built.

Fedor, thank you for trusting me with your mindset work, for bringing me on the incredible journey of 2015-2016, and then helping me to build-out Primed Mind, so we could share this with the world.

Phil Galfond, thank you for the eloquent foreword, for having faith in the process, for setting an incredible goal with The Galfond Challenge, and for bringing me along for the ride. The final day of your VeniVidi challenge will be one I remember forever.

Thank you to Scott Blumstein for bringing me in to help with the WSOP 2017 Final Table. It was a once-in-a-lifetime experience! Adrian Attenborough, what a ride, getting second in the 2022 WSOP Main Event after an incredible final table performance!

Chalie Hook, what a journey, looking forward to your book in the future…

A big thank you to all of the players kind enough to share their stories in this book: Kevin Martin, BERRI SWEET, Brian Rast, Kristen Foxen, Alex Foxen, Jason Koon, Matt Berkey, Ben CB, Jon Van Fleet, Lara Eisenburg. It's humbling, and you were all so kind to share.

There have been so many clients and supporters over the years who've helped my journey in poker, sharing their experiences with friends and sometimes publicly, unfortunately I'm going to forget some people, I'm sure, but please know that I'm grateful for the help (there are also many of you whom I know prefer to remain private, but please know I appreciate your help tremendously). Thanks also to Rob Tinnion, Alex Carr, Patrick Leonard, Gavin, Phil "the businessman' Karsen, Eric Crain, Rory Young, Sean Kapul, Blake Eastman, Lacey Jones, Georgie, Chris Kruk, Ana Marquez, Katie Stone, Jen Shahade,

Ryan Mcathron, Haralabos Voulgaris, Olivier Busquet, Sam Vousden, Michael Addamo, Will Jaffe, Matt Korbalas, Marc Alioto, Shakti Chauhan, Mark Herm, Nick Howard, Patrick Howard, Jason Koonce, Ivan Stokes, Larry, Jamie Kerstetter, Jeff Gross, Muskan Sethi, Ben Heath, Boris Kolev, Sam Grafton, Wayne Yap, Raghav Bansel, Bradley Ruben, Thomas Muhlocker, Michael Acevedo, Josh Arieh, Zach Elwood, Filipe Oliveira, Nuno Ascensao, Eric Worre.

Thanks to the coaches, hypnotherapists and experts who've trained me over the years. Without your knowledge, I wouldn't be the coach I am today.

Thank you to my excessive personal team for helping me stay "primed"... Lana Gerhing thanks for making me do all those pull ups, I appreciate you... Nick Eubanks, Mike Brown, Amanda Brundrett, Brendan Moore, Scott DeMoulin, Dan Fleyshman thanks for pushing me out of my comfort zone! Valentina, Meaghan, Samm, Natalie thanks for keeping my mind and body on track. Mollie Eastman, thanks for your help making me a sleep ninja. Christian, Jim, AJ, Dan, Stephen, Alex, Paul, Victoria - I appreciate you all.

Finally, I'd like to thank my peers in the industry whose excellent books I recommend, Tommy Angelo, Jared Tendler and Trica Cardner—if you haven't read them go check them out.

About the Authors

Elliot Roe

Elliot Roe is a leading mindset and performance coach, celebrated for elevating the mental game in poker. With a foundation in hypnotherapy, Elliot has developed 'Primed Mind,' an app acclaimed for helping players achieve peak performance. His expertise is not limited to poker; he also advises high performers across various disciplines, from UFC fighters & Olympians, to CEOs, Founders, and Hedge Fund Managers. Elliot's holistic approach to mindset and performance has positioned him as a pivotal figure for those seeking to conquer stress, enhance focus, and master the emotional complexities inherent to high-stakes decision-making, both on and off the felt. Learn more at ElliotRoe.com.

Ryan Carter

Ryan Carter is the CEO of Mindset Coach LLC and Primed Mind USA. As a former professional poker player, the height of his poker success came shortly after he began working with Elliot as a client. Ryan claimed 2nd in the 2012 WCOOP Main Event, making his claim to fame in the poker world as the guy who let "I won't million" happen.

Having always been a strong advocate for the importance of mindset for poker players, Ryan seized the opportunity to bring this content to the mainstream. The pair joined forces, and a decade later, they continue to build and expand that vision.